Exodus

Exodus

Why Americans Are Fleeing
Liberal Churches for
Conservative Christianity

Dave Shiflett

SENTINEL

SENTINEL
Published by the Penguin Group
Penguin Group (USA) Inc., 375 Hudson Street,
New York, New York 10014, U.S.A.
Penguin Group (Canada), 10 Alcorn Avenue,Toronto, Ontario, Canada M4V 3B2
(a division of Pearson Penguin Canada Inc.)
Penguin Books Ltd, 80 Strand, London WC2R 0RL, England
Penguin Ireland, 25 St. Stephen's Green, Dublin 2, Ireland
(a division of Penguin Books Ltd)
Penguin Books Australia Ltd, 250 Camberwell Road, Camberwell,
Victoria 3124, Australia (a division of Pearson Australia Group Pty Ltd)
Penguin Books India Pvt Ltd, 11 Community Centre, Panchsheel Park,
New Delhi–110 017, India
Penguin Group (NZ), Cnr Airborne and Rosedale Roads, Albany,
Auckland 1310, New Zealand (a division of Pearson New Zealand Ltd)
Penguin Books (South Africa) (Pty) Ltd, 24 Sturdee Avenue,
Rosebank, Johannesburg 2196, South Africa

Penguin Books Ltd, Registered Offices: 80 Strand, London WC2R 0RL, England

First published in 2005 by Sentinel, a member of Penguin Group (USA) Inc.

10 9 8 7 6 5 4 3 2 1

CIP data available

ISBN 1-59523-007-6

Printed in the United States of America
Set in Janson
Designed by Joseph Rutt

To the Peach, the boys, and my parents

Acknowledgments

My initial desire had been to write a book explaining why moderate alcohol, tobacco, and red meat consumption enhances and extends life. The working title was to be *Ripeness Is All*, after the Bard's wise observation, and I hoped to offer a pleasing alternative to those who champion wine by the thimbleful and the unlit cigar.

Bernadette Malone, my editor at Sentinel, suggested moving that idea to the back burner and taking up another weighty topic: the slide of liberal Protestantism and the advance of more conservative versions of the Christian faith. I had some experience in writing about religion, knew some interesting stories to tell, and also had a few unaired opinions on these matters. I took to the task with backing from Bernadette and her new imprint. Bernadette saw the manuscript through its various revisions, pruning bad jokes, antic metaphors, and lame allusions. For all this I thank her, and I hope to work with her again.

My wife, Susan, aka the Peach mentioned in the dedication, was her usual glorious self, showing great patience as I reported and wrote this book, all the while ignoring leaking skylights, a disintegrating roof and driveway, plus similar threats to hearth and home. Early readers Wlady Pleszycenski and Doug LeBlanc brought to my attention various errors and lapses in taste and style. The work of Megan Casey, Jennifer Paré, Cindy Buck, Susan Gamer, and Bruce Giffords at Sentinel is also greatly appreciated.

The writing was mostly done various places around Richmond, Virginia, including the library at Union Theological Seminary, a mainstay of the mainline. If staff members had known what I was up to, perhaps they would not have been so helpful and kind. Many thanks, in any case. Other writing, planning, and pondering were undertaken at O'Toole's, Legend Brewing Company, the Cary Street Café, Joe's Inn, and several city parks, where the wonders of the laptop came fully into flower.

I am also deeply thankful to all my readers.

Contents

Introduction

"We have figured out your problem. You're the only one here who believes in God."

In many contexts this would not be an alarming statement. Religious believers, especially those whose faith is readily apparent, can make some people uneasy, especially those with little or no religious belief.

As it happens, these words were spoken to a seminary student I know, while he was eating lunch in the seminary cafeteria. They were spoken by another seminary student, who was reflecting the views of fellow students and faculty.

Something has gone decidedly amiss when a person who believes in God is the odd man out at a seminary. Consider the problem in economic terms. The Christian religion, like most religions, is about the business of "selling God." That is the product Christians bring to the marketplace. The seminarian who doesn't believe in God, or the priest who has whittled down the deity to fit his own intellectual passions, can be likened to a biologist who insists that the Earth is six thousand years old and that every creature sprang from the ether fully formed. These are interesting ideas in their own way, but we shall go elsewhere to learn our biology. That is exactly what is happening throughout the Protestant mainline, and that is what this book is about: Americans are vacating progressive pews and flocking to churches that offer more traditional versions of Christianity.

We have, thankfully, come far from the day when skeptical clerics were rushed to the stake, or at the very least banished to some distant backwater. In our day, celebrity heretics (by traditionalist standards) have done quite well, as reflected in book sales and speaking fees. Bishop John Shelby Spong's vigorous rejection of traditional Christian belief has set cash registers to ringing throughout the world. He is hardly alone. But he and other progressive clerics have found themselves increasingly lonely over the past several decades. To again employ economic terms, they have lost market share. Their sermons may be brilliant, and to their minds highly relevant, as they take up the most contentious subjects of the day: war and peace, homosexuality, economic justice, the importance of recycling. Yet they have made a profound miscalculation. Most people don't go to church to learn the minister's opinions on whatever happens to be in the headlines. They can get similar opinions sitting on their sofas watching television, quite possibly presented by someone much better-looking.

Most people go to church to get something they cannot get elsewhere. This consuming public—people who already believe, or who are attempting to believe, or who want their children to believe—go to church to learn about the mysterious Truth on which the Christian religion is built. They want the Good News, not the minister's political views or intellectual coaching. The latter creates sprawling vacancies in the pews. Indeed, those empty pews can be considered the earthly reward for abandoning heaven, traditionally understood. As Adam Smith might put it, a hidden hand appears to work in religion as in economics.

The statement about belief in God that opens this book was actually spoken in the lunchroom of the Church Divinity School of the Pacific in Berkeley, California. It was spoken to Andy Ferguson, who at the time was somewhat under the impression that one went to seminary to learn about God, not to learn to disbelieve in God. Andy had once considered becoming an Episcopal priest. His Episcopal seminary experience helped cure him of that. He is today a highly regarded journalist, with whom we will visit at length in chapter 4. He is also a Catholic of fairly recent vintage. To reemploy our economic theme, he switched brands. And it seems safe to say he won't be switching back.

Andy Ferguson is part of a significant exodus out of what are still called the mainline churches—the Episcopal, Presbyterian, United Methodist, Church of Christ, and non–Southern Baptist churches predominant among them. The Episcopal Church, whose ongoing demise is the focus of the first two chapters, has lost a majority of its members. As we shall see, there may now be twice as many lesbians in the United States as Episcopalians. Substantial decline has struck the other denominations as well. Once populous and influential, they are increasingly beside the point, except as a subject for news stories about the decline of mainline Protestantism.

There is a counterpart to their decline, of course. As the mainline has moved closer to flatlining, churches that have maintained allegiance to traditional Christian belief, comparatively speaking, have experienced membership increases. Some of those increases are quite dramatic. The old-time religion not only survives but prevails. The most recent "Religious Congregations and Membership" study, published in 2000 by the Glenmary Research Center (the study is conducted each decade), tells the statistical story. If we take the losers first, we find that the Presbyterian Church USA (11,106 churches) has experienced a decline of 11.6 percent over the previous ten years; the United Methodist Church (35,721 churches) was down 6.7 percent; and the Episcopal Church (7,314 churches) lost 5.3 percent of its membership. Also, the United

Churches of Christ (5,863 churches) declined 14.8 percent, while the American Baptist Churches USA were down 5.7 percent.

The denominations showing the most congregational growth included the deeply conservative Southern Baptist Convention, a collection of 41,514 churches whose overall growth rate was 5 percent. The traditionalist Presbyterian Church in America (as opposed to the mainline Presbyterian Church USA) experienced an impressive 42.4 percent increase, while the Christian and Missionary Alliance rose 21.8 percent. Meanwhile, the Evangelical Free Church was up 57.2 percent, and Pentecostal denominations also boomed. The Assemblies of God, with 11,880 churches, saw 18.5 percent growth, while the Church of God, with 5,612 churches, saw growth of 40.2 percent. In the same spirit, Conservative Christian Churches and Churches of Christ, with 5,471 churches total, saw a membership increase of 18.6 percent.

What is behind traditionalist rise and progressive decline? The *New York Times*, in its summary of the survey, noted that "socially conservative churches that demand high commitment from their members grew faster than other religious denominations in the last decade." Glenmary director Ken Sanchagrin told the paper he was "astounded to see that by and large the growing churches are those that we ordinarily call conservative. And when I looked at those that were declining, most were moderate or liberal churches. And the more liberal the denomination, by most people's definition, the more they were losing." Mark Tooley, from the conservative Institute on Religion and Democracy, added: "Churches that are faithful to their historic teachings, that offer transcendent truth to their congregants, that demand something morally of their people, and that believe in the need for personal conversion have a strong incentive to grow. Churches that allow themselves to be defined by the secular culture's definition of 'inclusivity' and 'tolerance' really have little to offer that will change hearts or inspire great loyalty, much less create membership growth." The *Times*, whose pages are generally not accorded the same level of credibility as Scripture, at least by conservative believers, appears to be on target in this instance. Its findings closely echoed many other analyses of decline, including Thomas C. Reeve's *The Empty Church: Does Organized Religion Matter Anymore?* (1996) and Dean M. Kelley's *Why Conservative Churches Are Growing* (1986). These two works are widely respected, and their arguments are largely borne out by the reporting presented in this book.

Reeves, who writes from the perspective of a mainline Episcopalian, reminds us that ascendancy and decline are not peculiar to our time. The eighteenth-century Church of England, for example, "drank deeply of the Enlightenment and suffered from apathy and irreligion as a result." The 1740–1830 period saw such a decline that "the church was in danger of becoming a minority religious establishment." Religious dormancy, however, was shaken off by "great awakenings" and renewed religious enthusiasm. After World War II, church construction rose from $76 million in 1946 to $409 million by 1950 and over $1 billion by the end of the 1950's. Church membership rose from 70 million to over 100 million between 1945 and 1955, Reeves writes. Yet by the mid- to late 1960s, the story had dramatically changed. Gallup found in 1968 that 67 percent of Americans believed religion was losing its impact on society, a number that rose to 75 percent over the next few years. In a 1971 poll, nearly 40 percent of Catholic and Protestant clergy under forty had given serious thought to leaving the ministry. In 1985, Reeves adds, one-third of Methodist churches performed no baptisms; two-thirds did not offer membership classes. A 1995 study found that the Methodist churches had been losing one thousand members a week for the past thirty years.

Conservative churches, however, were growing. In 1967 the Southern Baptists, whom we shall visit in chapter 6, became America's largest non-Catholic religious body. The Baptist ascendancy was marked by a bitter internal struggle between traditionalists and progressives that the progressives lost. By the mid-1990s, the Southern Baptists were taking on 750 members and five churches per week. Elsewhere that decade the Assemblies of God grew 121 percent, Seventh-Day Adventists 92 percent, Church of God 183 percent, and Church of Nazarene 63 percent.

What explains the mainstream slide and the traditionalist surge?

Reeves concludes that a primary reason progressive churches continue to lose members is that they increasingly resemble social service agencies. "Liberal Protestantism in particular has become so secularized and indistinct that it cannot compete successfully with an abundance of causes and activities that many find more valuable," Reeves explains. While some mainline partisans blame a more "skeptical" age whose skepticism is the result of rising education levels, Reeves agrees with a Gallup survey that found that while college graduates "treat religion with more skepticism," they are "far from hostile." A survey of Presbyterian baby boomers found that those "who lost their faith, or who adopted unorthodox opinions, did so before, not after, going to college." What diminished religious interest more than skepticism was a lack of fervor on the part of the churches themselves. "Somehow, in the course of the past century, these churches lost the will or the ability to teach the Christian faith and what it requires to a succession of younger cohorts in a way so as to command their allegiance."

Dean M. Kelley's explanation for the growth of conservative churches is similar, though Kelley puts the point more bluntly. Successful churches "are not 'reasonable,' they are not 'tolerant,' they are not ecumenical, they are not 'relevant,'" he insists. "Quite the contrary! They often refuse to recognize the validity of other

churches' teachings, ordinations, sacraments. They observe unusual rituals and peculiar dietary customs, such as foot-washing and
vegetarianism among Seventh-Day Adventists, abstention from
stimulants among Mormons. They disregard the 'decent opinions
of mankind' by persisting in irrational behavior, such as the Jehovah's Witnesses' refusal of blood transfusions. They try to impose
uniformity of belief and practice among members by censorship,
heresy trials, and the like."

Kelley cites a study by Professor George R. LaNoue Jr. of
Johns Hopkins University that compares membership in the liberal and conservative branches of several denominations between
1940 and 1968. Liberal churches, according to Kelley, are "more
urbanized and cosmopolitan. They enjoy greater influence and
mobility. Their members have more education on the average than
do those of conservative branches. One would expect them, therefore, to appeal more successfully to an increasingly urban, affluent,
educated and mobile population than could the conservative
branches, and thus to attract more members and grow more rapidly." Yet this was not the case, he found. Instead, "the conservative
branches are increasing proportionately more rapidly than the
liberal!"

Central to conservative church success, Kelley insists, is commitment to creed. He offers Mormonism as an example. Mormons remain deeply committed to their beliefs (which seem quite
bizarre to non-Mormons), just as they have always done. Their
predecessors withstood intense persecution and ridicule and undertook a mass migration in which they "polygamously populated
vast areas of the West, and persisted in polygamy for forty years
despite decisions of the U.S. Supreme Court and expeditions of
the U.S. Cavalry!" Today the Mormon religion continues to make
high demands on its members in both dietary matters and mis-

sionary work. It continues with religious practices and rituals that, as we shall see in our concluding chapter, will strike most Americans as quite extraordinary. And Mormonism is thriving.

An analysis of the Presbyterian Church USA by Benton Johnson, Dean R. Hoge, and Donald A. Luidens ("Mainline Churches: The Real Reason for Decline," *First Things*, March 1993) found that the best predictor of church participation is orthodox Christian belief, "especially the teaching that a person can be saved only through Jesus Christ. Virtually all our baby boomers who believe this are active members of a church."

Now, to this book.

Readers are hereby assured that this is not the work of a scholar or a particularly avid churchgoer. It does not pretend to reach even the outer limits of being an exhaustive work. As religion writer Terry Mattingly sensibly reminds us, the "God beat" is so vast and complex that taking on even the smallest aspect is a daunting task that is doomed to at least some degree of failure, and perhaps a high degree.

What I have done is to try to tell the story of mainline decline and traditionalist growth through the eyes of individuals on both sides of this divide. This book is not a creation of the study. There are statistics within, but not many. It largely comprises interviews with priests, priestesses, ministers, evangelists, refugees from the mainline, and a lawyer or two. It includes some brief excerpts from various edicts, memoirs, sermons, news articles, and diatribes. There are also personal reflections that have been compressed by the magic of ferocious editing.

The book is presented in two parts. Part One discusses current events in the mainline, beginning with the train wreck known as the Episcopal Church USA. It is commonly understood that the election of the Rt. Rev. Eugene Robinson, an openly gay priest, to be bishop of the diocese of New Hampshire was undertaken in clear opposition to traditional church teaching and Scripture. What is often left unsaid is that this was hardly the first time tradition had been trounced. The Rt. Rev. Robinson's sexual life was at issue and was accommodated, just as the Episcopal Church earlier found a way to embrace bishops who believe that Jesus is no more divine, at least in a supernatural sense, than Bette Midler. By my way of thinking, the Rt. Rev. Robinson has hardly been the most egregious sinner to be accommodated.

Nonetheless, many Americans, believers or not, reasonably wonder about the mechanism by which this denomination has cast overboard its traditions and the Scripture on which they are based. The questions I put to priests and supporters of these innovations were simple: How can you square these changes with your traditions? And do you have the slightest inkling that tampering with the Writ your forebears considered holy, and indeed the blueprint for eternal salvation, might have some negative consequences, and perhaps spectacularly negative consequences? I then traveled to the dissident camp, where traditionalists have decided to create a network of dissenting churches that will maintain Episcopal traditions, including a veneration for Scripture. My questions for the dissidents were two: Why are you departing over homosexuality when so many other departures from tradition have already been accommodated? Second, why was your denomination unable to maintain its traditions in the face of the progressive onslaught?

The Episcopal Church has of course supplied commentators with copy for many years, often because of its veneration for trends. In 1984, to give one well-known example, the proprietors of New York's Cathedral of St. John the Divine unveiled a crucifix featuring "Christa"—a female remake of Jesus that would likely have made Herod's sap rise. Yet the Episcopalians are hardly the only participants in this religious freak show, as we see in chapter 3. The Presbyterians, who have been fighting their own sex wars for decades (as have the Methodists and others), created large columns of refugees by embracing nontraditional ideas, including one insisting that the denomination transfer thousands of dollars from its collection plates into the pockets of Angela Davis—a vibrant apostle, to be sure, though of Karl Marx, not Jesus of Nazareth. The United Church of Christ's general synod endorsed homosexual ordinations in 1983, which was not so great an offense, to some at least, as were references to God as both Mother and Father (suggesting a supernatural sexual identity crisis) and the likening of the Almighty to "a Bakerwoman" and a grove of trees. Christian aesthetics have fallen far since the King James Version and Michelangelo.

While laughing at comical clerics is no small delight, chapter 3 has two more serious reasons for being. One is to show how nontraditional beliefs not only have permeated the mainline but are common among believers who are often portrayed as dangerous fundamentalists bent on a theocratic takeover of the local school board, if not all three branches of the federal government. These ranks include the dread born-again Christians, one component of the "lightly educated, easily led" storm troopers of the religious right. As we shall see, that canard is ridiculous at every level, unless one happens to raise funds for liberal causes. And while many Americans hold less than orthodox views, a strong majority believe that God is omnipotent and as such "rules this world." This is in much contrast to the "30 percent God" popular with some progressives, a deity who would have a difficult time fixing a parking ticket. For some progressives, even a 30 percent God—God Lite—is far too much. We depart this chapter, and Part One, from a Unitarian church service, where we hear the testimonial of a Unitarian chaplain who refused to give dying patients any hope that a better home awaited them. She simply didn't believe in God or an afterlife. We are left hoping the patients had enough breath to seek a second opinion.

The 100 percent God—the great I AM—continues to find a stronghold in traditionalist churches, which are the focus of this book's second section. Part Two largely comprises interviews with individuals who have either left the mainline or spent their religious lives defending and promoting Christian orthodoxy. My basic questions: Why did you leave the mainline, and what have you found on the other side? Andy Ferguson, the odd man out at the Episcopal seminary, gives us his Catholic perspective, as does conservative publisher Al Regnery. Father John McCloskey, perhaps our age's most successful Catholic evangelist, tells us why a liturgy established long before the age of reason continues to attract such highly educated and often profoundly skeptical people as Robert Bork and Robert Novak.

Chapter 5 takes us into the lesser-known world of Orthodoxy. Conservative writer Frederica Mathewes-Green and husband Gary Mathewes-Green tell why they left the Episcopal Church, where he was a priest, for this deeply mystical faith. Like most Americans, I knew little about this ancient church, whose services are unique, mysterious, and otherworldly—something like God is said to be. From there we travel to a Southern Baptist seminary, which is a far different world from an Orthodox service, and from an Episcopal seminary. The Southern Baptist belief in biblical inerrancy is said to be unpalatable to anyone who has gotten through middle school, yet we meet a longtime minister—he preached his first sermon at age sixteen—who went to Oxford with Bill Clinton. I wondered if these Baptists truly believe that mainline clerics who support gay ordination are bound for hell. Without revealing the answer, their expectations for what awaits their progressive counterparts are not pleasant. They also devoutly believe *Roe v. Wade* is not long for this world.

The orthodox, 100 percent God, the traditionalists tell us, does not have the world to Himself. He is opposed by a fallen angel named Satan, whose existence is also a matter of certitude among orthodox believers. Satan is given his due in chapter 7, where the evangelical response to the Columbine school massacre is presented by pastors who buried some of the dead. Those who believe in an omnipotent God face great struggle in the face of such horror: why would God allow such a thing to happen, especially to those who have done their best to conform themselves to His ways? The pastoral response, and the response of victims' families, makes clear that this serious God is worshiped by very serious people. This is not, as my editor likes to say, God Lite, but the Absolut God.

Satan is also a mainstay in prison sermons, as we find during a discussion with evangelist Charles Colson at the start of chapter 8. Colson is another born-again Christian who defies the stereotype: Boston born, Ivy League educated, and for a time (before his conversion, to be sure) the second most powerful man in the world, by some accounts. That Colson has dedicated the last several decades to ministering to a massive number of African Americans and other minorities not only makes him an American hero. He is also a reminder that conservative Christians are determined that their faith be projected into the future. Evangelizing can be considered religious procreation, and in this area conservatives are much more active than liberals.

We close with what Father McCloskey calls the "conversion of the century": Dr. Bernard Nathanson, who by his own count presided over sixty thousand abortions. He is now a conservative Catholic.

Those who write this type of book are reasonably asked about their religious views and prejudices. I classify myself as an itinerant Presbyterian, with an emphasis on the itinerant. I currently belong to no church, though sometimes I attend a mainline Presbyterian church close by my house. Location is indeed everything. I have never had much luck believing in angels or devils and tend to be not entirely comfortable with people who believe Eden's serpent actually spoke. I also have no dog in the Episcopalian fight. If that church wants to name chimpanzees to its vestry, that is its business, and I sense that sooner or later the thing will be done. When the rare person asks me if I believe something is a sin, my response is always the same: I did not write the moral codes, which were here long before I arrived and will be here long after I vanish. These days such questions tend to come during a discussion of homosexuality. My view tends to be that according to these codes homosexual behavior is a sin, but one sin among many. By these same codes, I have plenty of sins of my own, which neutralize me as an inquisitor. In addition, I make a point of not classifying people by their sexual practices, which I don't want to know and which, again in my opinion, are not the most important thing about a person, and certainly not central to anyone's being. All that said, it is also my view that as we celebrate our diversity of religious choices we might keep in mind that the ability to choose entails the possibility of choosing poorly, if not disastrously. If our minds are truly open on these matters, we should admit the possibility of a True Way that is illuminated accurately in Holy Writ, and therefore editing Scripture to the point of turning it on its head will have serious consequences.

In a more general sense, William James sounded familiar interior notes in his *Varieties of Religious Experience*. Those of a religious temperament, he wrote, share an array of beliefs, including a suspicion that "the visible world is part of a more spiritual universe from which it draws its chief significance" and that "the union or harmonious relation with the higher universe is our true end." He also notes an "uneasiness" in such people that he defines as "a sense that there is something wrong about us as we naturally stand" that is best addressed by religion. I have also appreciated James's view of religion as a biological function, especially when considering the idea that those who reject a vibrant and demanding religion that they could pass on to their children are, to some degree, courting their own genetic extinction: "Taking creeds and faith-state together, as forming 'religions,' and treating these as purely subjective phenomena, without regard to the question of their 'truth,' we are obliged, on account of their extraordinary influence upon action and endurance, to class them amongst the most important biological functions of mankind."

My other interest in religion is as a story, one that is immense and may be the biggest story of all, one that can only partially be told even by all those who would try to tell some portion of it. It is sometimes entirely frightening, as when we learn more about Islamic fundamentalism. At other times, it is intriguing, mystifying, entertaining, or a combination of all these characteristics and others besides.

That is certainly true regarding the ongoing attraction of religious traditionalism, sometimes for those who would not be considered likely suspects. Many readers of the *New York Post*, for instance, were one morning shocked to read that former Beatle John Lennon, who early in his stardom outraged traditionalists by proclaiming his band more popular than Jesus and later wrote the secular hymn "Imagine," had become a devout fan of none other than televangelist Pat Robertson, to the point of falling to his knees and touching the television screen, apparently in hope of receiving a supernatural lift from the flickering image. A similar story was found in the book *Nowhere Man*, in which author Robert Rosen informs us that in the late 1970s Lennon had taken to watching Billy Graham on TV. "At first he watched only for entertainment," Rosen wrote. "Then, one day, he had an epiphany—he allowed himself to be touched by the hand of Jesus Christ, and it drove him to tears of joy and ecstasy. He drew a picture of a crucifix: he was born again, and the experience was such a kick he had to share it with Yoko. John and Yoko sat in front of the TV watching Billy Graham sermons. Every other sentence out of John's mouth was 'Thank you, Jesus,' or 'Thank you, Lord.'"

These stories were denounced by some critics as fabrications, yet Lennon would not be the first popular icon to pursue the traditional version of Jesus. Bob Dylan's conversion to Christianity is well known and appears to be intact. Dylan was converted not by Unitarians but by the efforts of the vibrantly evangelical Vineyard ministry. Last year the *London Spectator* informed readers that Keith Richards, the Rolling Stones guitarist, goes to church from time to time and lives in a decidedly devout household. His wife Patti, wrote biographer Christopher Sandford, is a "devout Lutheran" who attends a weekly Bible study group and "won't stand for swearing around the house." At the time of their marriage, Patti's parents told reporters that Richards was an "enthusiastic disciple of Christ" who had "embraced Christ as a way of life." Meantime, a personal favorite, guitarist Jorma Kaukonen, formerly of the Jefferson Airplane, posted an entry in his Internet diary (January 4, 2004) telling his readers that he and his wife Vanessa, while visiting San Francisco, had "stopped in Old St. Mary's and heard the end of the morning Mass. I am not Catholic, but there is something tangibly powerful in tradition and ritual."

These days, in the United States, the religion story is often about division. There has always been friction within Christianity, and in our era the Body of Christ, as the spectrum of believers and practitioners is known, has been experiencing an ongoing stroke. Part of the Body is vibrant and growing; part is in the grip of advancing morbidity. The dynamic side, interestingly enough, is the more theologically conservative, holding fast to ancient creeds and writings revered as eternal, revealed Truth. The stricken side is the progressive side, which has tailored its message to more closely fit social development. This seems something of a paradox. In the natural world, adapting is central to survival, and so it would seem that the progressive versions of Christianity would have the advantage. Yet that is not the case.

Progressives remind us that Christianity has been profoundly malleable throughout its history, and all but supernaturally creative. The delineation of the Trinity may be the prime example. Such innovations have allowed Christianity to rise from its humble origins as a desert cult to become the greatest of world religions. Change is inevitable. It is good. And it rarely fails to cause controversy. Currently the flashpoint is homosexuality. Not long ago, female ordination rocked churches, as did abortion and the divorce/remarriage debates. The genius of Christianity (and especially Protestantism), progressives argue, has been its ability to eventually go with the flow. Declining membership is nothing more than the chaff departing the wheat. An interesting view for any institution, and especially one that lives off donations, but one apparently widely held.

My first stop was at the progressive camp. St. John's Episcopal Church in Richmond, Virginia, is one of the most famous Episcopal churches in the nation. It was here in 1775 that Patrick Henry issued his ringing proclamation: "Give me liberty, or give me death." The Episcopal Church, by freeing itself from many of its traditional beliefs, sometimes appears to be well on its way to achieving both.

Part One

Our Proud Illusions

One

The Episcopalians

In the Name of Tolerance

One Tuesday in latter-day Christendom, the sun rose in the east, the sky became a pleasant blue, and the Episcopal Church USA approved a gay man as bishop for its small New Hampshire diocese. The news accounts from Minneapolis, where this momentous event occurred, pointed out that the Rt. Rev. Eugene Robinson was a noncelibate gay, which would indicate a dedication to a cause and also put him at odds with the accepted policy of welcoming celibate homosexuals into the priesthood. The Rt. Rev. Robinson had some fourteen years previously left his wife and two daughters to pursue his new life, and so the Episcopalian hierarchy was putting the church on a new path: consecrating homosexuals who openly rejected, at the time of their consideration, traditional Episcopal teaching against sex outside of marriage.

The ascendancy of the Rt. Rev. Robinson, who is apparently much beloved by those who know him, was not a great surprise. The modern Episcopal Church USA is all but unrivaled in its willingness to accommodate itself to cultural change. It had a few decades previously decided that divorce and remarriage are acceptable, not adulterous, as indicated by Jesus and church tradition. It had accepted women into the priesthood as well, no doubt sending Saint Paul spinning in his grave. It is also true that the Episcopal Church believes strongly in representative democracy, and by many accounts the Rt. Rev. Robinson represents a significant sexual segment of the Episcopal priesthood. Louie Crew, founder of the Episcopal gay organization Integrity, told the *New York Times* that as many as 20 percent of all Episcopal priests are gay or lesbian. There is a suspicion that there may be more gay Episcopalians than Republican Episcopalians.

While the elevation of the Rt. Rev. Robinson was lauded for "widening the circle" and promised to attract new members to the declining denomination (in 1995 Episcopal priest Alexander Seabrook insisted that "every time that we ordain someone who is not a heterosexual white male, we gain hundreds of new members"), his good fortune was a pill too bitter for some traditionalists to swallow. They quickly went about the business of establishing a network of dissenting churches and called for oversight from bishops associated with the worldwide Anglican Communion, of which the Episcopal Church is a very small part. Some traditionalists had earlier departed when the church ordained women, while some hung on. These latter-day traditionalists had bent to many winds over the years, but they would not bend for Bishop Robinson. Exodus, they concluded, was their only reasonable course of action. This historic denomination was splintering before our eyes.

The decision by traditionalists to leave their mother church quickly became the scandalous aspect of the Episcopal drama. Such is the reactionaries' reward. Their decision to form a network of dissenting churches, thus leaving perhaps the best brand name in Protestantism, also raised questions among those who might otherwise sympathize with their plight. Why had they drawn the line at the consecration of Gene Robinson? While it is true that traditional Episcopal teaching reflects Old and New Testament admonitions against homosexuality, traditionalist Episcopalians had put up with much worse in their bishops for decades, including public rejection of many if not most foundational beliefs. If traditionalists could remain in a church whose bishops loudly and repeatedly rejected the divinity of Christ and His bodily resurrection, why couldn't they live with a mild-mannered homosexual living with a long-term partner in remote New Hampshire? Who more mocks Jesus's terrible suffering and sublime sacrifice than a bishop who openly dismisses the Easter Hope?

In the next chapter, I will put those questions to leading traditionalists who have lost their denomination to their progressive brethren. This chapter takes up the story of the winners, who have raised important questions of their own: How do you square homosexuality with Scripture and traditional church teaching, which view homosexuality as sharing the same divine displeasure as matricide? Is everything negotiable these days? And is it even slightly possible that there could be significant eternal risks in tampering with what Christians through the ages have considered "God's blueprint" for human salvation? These questions are appropriate not only for the Episcopal Church. They have relevance throughout the Protestant mainline.

The Episcopal Church's gay wars did not begin in Minneapolis, or anywhere near Minneapolis. In 1977 New York Bishop Paul Moore ordained the denomination's first openly homosexual priest. In the 1990s, Bishop John Shelby Spong of Newark, New Jersey, undertook a vibrant campaign of gay advocacy; one of his assistants, the Rt. Rev. Walter Righter, also ordained a gay deacon, inspiring conservatives to instigate a heresy trial in 1996, a bellwether event taken up in the next chapter. By the time Gene Robinson stood for consecration, the beaches had been thoroughly softened. He prevailed by a vote of sixty-two bishops for, forty-five against. In a presidential race, that would qualify as a landslide.

Post-consecration stories were filled with statements from church leaders expressing their desire for "healing" and "harmony" and perhaps "reconciliation" as well, reminding some of us that religious professionals are unrivaled in their ability to wring their hands and write press releases simultaneously, likely with at least a few fingers crossed. There seemed little prospect for harmony or reconciliation. Neither side appeared to truly desire either. This was not only a divorce but an upheaval, a journey across the Rubicon and perhaps the Styx as well. One set of certitudes had been replaced by another set of certitudes. Little but bad blood could be left in the wake, no matter what the Episcopal front office insisted.

I wanted to know how deep the real passions ran as well as how the winners justified jettisoning twenty centuries of Christian morality. Indeed, I wondered exactly how they did so: what exactly is the mechanism for convincing the believing rank and file to ignore not only their own church traditions but Scripture they have been taught was written by the very hand of God? The best place to find straight answers was likely to be not in the front office but on the front lines. I needed to talk to some priests. Taking into account the prevailing liberalism of the Episcopal clergy, it seemed a safe bet that finding a priest who was certain not only that the Robinson consecration was right but that opposition was deeply wrong and driven by impure motives would be no problem. As it happened, the first priest I phoned fit the bill.

The Rev. Bruce Gray is rector at St. John's Episcopal Church in Richmond, Virginia, where Patrick Henry gave his famous speech in 1775, with many eminences in the audience, including Thomas Jefferson. Henry, Jefferson, and their partners in rebellion maintain a strong presence in this part of the country. Nearby, in a bar district called Shockoe Slip, a warehouse under renovation bears the message that Jefferson's "Virginia Statute for Religious Freedom" was first presented and debated on that site. Richmond's metropolitan area hosts around two dozen Episcopal churches, and Virginia is the denomination's largest diocese, with 189 churches total. St. John's, a small church made of white wood, sits atop Church Hill, surrounded by graves.

Rector Gray warmly greeted me in his cozy office just beyond the shadow of St. John's steeple, which was not part of the church when Henry held forth, he told me. Rector Gray was quick to point out that he was married and had come to Richmond by way of Albany, New York, where even during the Vietnam era the level of civility within the church was much higher than it is now. He had a comfortable appearance and manner, wearing light slacks and a sport shirt, and was pleasantly devoted to the blessings of the dinner table, a disposition we shared. He was also very fast to the job of raising doubts and suspicions about the conservative forces that were by then in full retreat.

These dissidents, he began, were not only forming a network of refugee churches, which is bad enough. They had announced their intention to bring in African bishops to provide oversight for their renegade network. Though Rector Gray did not mention it, this is something of a cosmic irony. The Episcopal Church is noted for its wealthy, white membership; the communion cup represents the only blood in its sanctuaries that isn't blue. Now, in order to preserve its traditions, traditionalists were calling on black Africans to rescue them. One might suggest a bit of karma at work.

Rector Gray was not interested in karma, or irony either. Instead, he wanted me to know that there was something unsettling and perhaps nefarious about these African bishops and their American petitioners. The Network of Anglican Communion Dioceses and Parishes, as the dissident churches were calling themselves, is not simply a group of conservative Episcopalians who may take their Scripture and the church's ancient traditions a bit too seriously, Gray indicated. The more important and less well known truth is that the NACDP works in "secrecy," especially regarding its funding. "Some of the major funding for the NACDP appears to be coming from an individual who has supported reactionary political and religious causes," Rector Gray said. This unnamed person "has said that he supports turning the United States into a theocracy governed by biblical law." That wasn't all. "Some of these same funders are supplying the resources for the African and Southern Hemisphere bishops to come to various conservative meetings. It is fair to ask if the same effort, resources, and commitment are being put into the heterosexual AIDS pandemic in Africa, and if not, why not?"

Those are serious charges. Having a financial backer who shares theological and political views with, among others, the late Francisco Franco and who hopes to place America under theocratic rule is not likely to be well received by the Episcopal rank and file—or by Baptists either, for that matter. At the same time, the idea of an Episcopal-led theocracy is comical. If the council had indeed convinced a billionaire that it might play a role in such a coup, his was a well-deserved fleecing. Rector Gray did not confide the name of this dark presence, though he was likely referring to either Howard Ahmanson Jr. or Richard Mellon Scaife, who has been linked to the council in other reports. Scaife, it might be mentioned, had established his bona fides by funding earlier efforts to bring down Bill Clinton. But if comical, the fact that Rector Gray shared these suspicions underscores the political nature of the Episcopal combat. Demonizing the opposition, after all, is one of the chief arrows in the political operative's quiver. It is not usually thought to be part of the Christian witness.

Rector Gray had not made these allegations only to a visiting writer. In a series of sermons prior to the consecration vote, he raised the specter of the theocratic billionaire and also insisted that he and his pro-consecration colleagues occupied the "middle ground" in this dispute, which by default places the opposition in the moral and intellectual low country. "It is becoming far easier to affiliate with those on the right or the left who are so certain that they are correct in all matters political and theological," he told his congregation. "It doesn't require much thinking. Our own worst fears are supported and encouraged. We don't have to deal with those who disagree with us, thereby avoiding intellectual honesty and hard work."

This formulation is familiar to anyone who follows political disputes. It is triune in nature—positing that persons occupy a left, middle, or right position—but, as is often the case, one position in this trinity does not actually exist. The first person could be said to be the right, whose position is non-consecration. Rector Gray is pro-consecration, which he casts as the centrist position, or in this scheme the second person. But who represents the third person? Rector Gray indicated that would be the "left," but one must wonder how the leftist position might differ from the centrist one. Not only does Rector Gray have no enemies on the left, but there really is no leftist position.

A little sleight of hand is to be expected, of course, as was another charge Rector Gray took from the political playbook: those on the opposition side are mean people. Virginia's bishop had been treated badly by anti-consecration Episcopalians because he voted for Robinson's consecration, Rector Gray said. An invitation to visit a conservative church had been withdrawn, and he had been publicly denounced during a church gathering. There was only one angel in that drama. "Even when he was referred to in a public meeting as a 'demon' and as 'Satan,' he maintained his patience and, for the most part, responded firmly, but gently," Rector Gray said.

Rector Gray's viewpoint had been found acceptable by his small (under two hundred) congregation, he said, two-thirds of

whom he considered "traditionalist." One member had asked that
his donations be used strictly at St. John's. That was the extent of
the dissent, at least on Church Hill. Rector Gray was not sure what
effect the AAC rebellion would have on the denomination as a
whole, though he had the calm demeanor of a man who knows he
is on the winning side.

But there is more to all this than politics. Did Rector Gray en-
tertain the slightest worry that converting a former sin into a
celebrated and even consecrated virtue might possibly have eternal
consequences? Was rewriting the historic teachings of a church—
teachings based on what was once believed to be the Word of
God—of no greater consequence than rewriting the bylaws of the
Ruritan Club?

Rector Gray was ready for these questions, which he had addressed in his pre-Minneapolis sermons. "Jesus never said a word
that's recorded in the Bible about homosexuality, one way or the
other," he said. "He did, however, condemn the practice of divorce. It would appear that Jesus was seeking to protect the place
of women in society. In this regard he took a very radical position
vis-à-vis his own culture. Now one group in the church is vigor-
ously condemning the election and presumed consecration of a gay
man living in a long-term committed relationship, but no one, to
my knowledge, has condemned the election of the new bishop of
Arizona, who has been divorced, remarried, and who has children
from his previous marriage. Why? Because our culture and church
have come to accept the reality and pain of divorce and provided a
means, even in the church, to bring God's love and reconciliation
to bear in such difficult moments."

I assured Rector Gray that I am no theologian but am familiar
with the teaching, attributed to Jesus, that those who divorce and
remarry are guilty of adultery. Isn't this the same Jesus, I asked,
who is also on record as saying that to even think about sleeping

with one's neighbor's wife is as bad as the act itself? Could it be true that this same Jesus believes it is permissible and indeed salutary for two men, even two men in a long-term relationship, to have sex? The real problem, I suggested, is not only that Jesus set a very high sexual standard, but that it is one few humans could ever hope to live by.

Rector Gray agreed that the standard is high. What I did not seem to understand, and what he hoped to show me, was that these issues had been considered by very thoughtful people who had come to conclusions far different from, not to mention far more humanitarian than, the traditions so dear to their opponents.

Bishop Peter Lee of Virginia, for example, had addressed these issues in a letter to his fellow believers. He had taken the Scriptural issue head-on: "Many people believe any homosexual activity is clearly prohibited by scripture," the bishop wrote. "The seven verses scattered through the Bible that mention homosexual behavior are all negative. But other Christians who take scripture seriously believe that the Biblical writers were not addressing the realities of people with a permanent homosexual orientation living in faithful, monogamous relationships, and that the relevant scriptural support for those relationships is similar to the expectations of faithfulness scripture places on marriage."

Rector Gray said he shared the bishop's view, and he handed me another document from a thoughtful clergyman. "You might think that if we want to know what the Bible says about a particular topic all we have to do is look it up, see what it says and then apply it," the writer began. "The snag is that that method of reading scripture can lead to problems, e.g. Exodus 21:15 reads, 'whoever hits his father or mother shall be put to death,' Exodus 21:17 reads 'whoever curses his father or mother shall be put to death.' Deuteronomy 25:11–12 says 'a woman who tried to protect her husband in a fight by seizing his enemy's genitals should have her hand cut off.' Deuteronomy 21:18–21 says 'a stubborn rebellious boy who drinks and eats to excess and refuses to obey his parents should be stoned to death.'" An additional problem, the writer added, is that many "Christians in fact quoted Scripture to defend slavery against those who wished to abolish it," and closer to our day, the Episcopal Church in Nigeria "allows polygamy because it is found in the Bible whereas we in the West believe in monogamous marriage relationships."

I had read this sort of thing before. In fact, had Rector Gray read this document aloud, I might have mistaken it for the work of Christopher Hitchens, the brilliant essayist, table-pounding atheist, and author of perhaps the only book-length attack on Mother Teresa (*The Missionary Position*). It turned out that Hitchens was not the author of the document Rector Gray had given me. It had instead been penned by the Bishop of Wales.

The bishop had provided a blueprint of the mechanism by which Scriptural admonitions are neutralized. The process is quite simple. Step one is to find a passage in the Old Testament that is startling in its brutality—cutting off limbs, executing unruly children, and stoning women are popular choices. Step two is to find the New Testament passage one wants to undermine—in this case, passages critical of homosexuality, and before that admonitions against divorce and remarriage and female ordination. Step three is to insist that if one is indeed taking one's cues from the Bible, then one must take the book all in all. Ergo: opposing homosexuality is no less extreme than stoning annoying children. The Old Testament thus neutralizes the New and leaves wide the way for the substitute virtues, such as tolerance, inclusion, and the insistence that sexual behavior traditionally considered sinful is to be considered morally co-equal with heterosexual monogamy.

Rector Gray suggested a sermon by another local Episcopal priest that touched all the progressive bases in a clear and concise manner. The Rev. Robert G. Hertherington had delivered this sermon prior to the Minneapolis vote, and it can be considered an excellent example of the type of pro-consecration sermon given around the nation, and also the type of sermon that has driven traditionalists from the church. Its reasoning purports to be theological; it will strike other readers as being based not on theology but on the argument from the slippery slope.

This sermon also began by noting the seven Scriptural references to sex between men. All are against it, the Rev. Hertherington agreed, and as a result some people "feel that this is enough evidence to refuse consent for Bishop Robinson's election." Yet the Rev. Hertherington had taken a closer look and found hairs worth splitting. "The references are to specific sexual activities between men. In one instance there is opposition to casual sex between men. Another is opposition to a form of temple prostitution between men. Apparently some religious traditions in the ancient world considered sexual ecstasy as part of the religious path to God. St. Paul clearly condemned this activity."

The problem with Paul and his colleagues, the Rev. Hertherington continued, was that they didn't fully understand what it was they were condemning. "No one in the ancient world thought of homosexual orientation as a natural way of living," he explained. "In the eyes of the ancient world homosexual activity was unnatural and should be condemned as a sin. Today some would argue that homosexual orientation is part of the order of nature. As a result, it should be accepted. Today, some people who are homosexual seek to live in life-long, monogamous and faithful relationships with their partners. This was an idea which the writers of scripture never imagined. In this light we could argue that scripture is silent about lifelong, faithful relationships between people of the same sex."

This passage may strike some readers as curious. The notion

that antiquity knew less about homosexuality than we might presume to know and that the ancients were less accepting of homosexuality than we are today is not convincing. Athens and Sparta were part of the ancient world. Enough said, one hopes. Additionally, the idea that gay people have only recently become interested in faithful relationships also rings parochial.

Having dismissed biblical teachings on sexual sin as being based on ignorance, the Rev. Hertherington then turned to the task of substituting preferred values. "What about justice?" he said. "All people should have the same opportunities in God's world. What about the concept of hospitality? Since all of us are created in the image of God, we should offer hospitality to all God's creatures. These avenues could provide a positive path through scripture that would affirm the blessing of same sex relationships."

The Rev. Hertherington disagreed strongly with those who argue that gay consecration stands outside Episcopal tradition. The thing one must remember about tradition, he suggested, was that the "traditions of the church have changed over time. Take the role of women, for example. Women have only been part of the ordained ministry in the Episcopal Church for the last twenty-five years. Now in the American Episcopal church, women can be deacons, priests and bishops. That is a big change. It should be noted that this role for women has not been totally accepted throughout the Anglican Communion. So it has not been a deal breaker for the other provinces which do not accept women the way we do." He then played what might be called the Bishop of Arizona card regarding divorce and remarriage: "So you can see over the years the traditions of the church have changed. Perhaps our attitude toward openly homosexual people who are living in committed relationships should change as well."

He ended by praising the Rt. Rev. Robinson for his openness. "The people of the Diocese of New Hampshire took into account that aspect of his personality and incorporated it into a larger view. This led to the conclusion that he was the best person for the job. In fact, in the meetings before the election took place in New Hampshire the nominees for bishop brought their spouses to meet and greet members of the diocese. While others brought wives or husbands, Gene brought his partner. Gene has been very straightforward in presenting himself."

The Rev. Hertherington presented the progressive case clearly and concisely and in the process showed himself and his position to be fully enlightened and humane. He called for broad-mindedness, justice, equality, and hospitality. He praised openness and also reminded his listeners that, so far as tradition goes, the Episcopal Church had, over the past quarter-century or so, embraced a tradition of overturning traditions.

By another reading, he simply argued that the denomination has long been sliding down the slippery slope. So why not slide a little further and consecrate gays? Why single them out for exclusion?

These, to my mind, are excellent questions, and they'll be left to the traditionalists we'll meet in the next chapter. For the moment, however, these few documents, presented as representative of the progressive case, make it clear that the contemporary virtues of openness, inclusion, hospitality, and tolerance have won out over biblical admonition, especially regarding sexual sin. The rout has been total. The Rev. Hertherington provided, though perhaps not intentionally, the reasoning that justifies this profound readjustment. His sermon is clearly based on the assumption that Scripture is merely the work of its authors, whose writing necessarily reflects the biases of their age and culture. Traditionalists of course have a far different view: the Bible is not a human diary; it is God's revelation, which is the only reason it should be taken seriously. If the Bible is merely a collection of human thoughts, imaginings, and desires, the atheists are right—it is a contemptible piece of literature, perhaps the most contemptible ever constructed. It has inspired untold millions of people to put themselves and others through immense suffering, and sometimes death, in pursuit of a ludicrous and indeed nonexistent salvation. This is, after all, the religion that has traditionally taught that if one's eye interferes with the gaining of salvation, one must pluck it out. The sinning hand must be severed. Sin must be isolated and destroyed, lest it destroy individuals and communities.

Before leaving Richmond, I wanted to get one more view, this time from a woman. Despite much commentary to the contrary, my experience indicated that men and women often do see things differently. The Rev. Sandra Levy was rector of St. Mark's Episcopal Church, a congregation with a significant gay contingent. I wondered how her congregation as a whole was taking these developments, and how she squared her support for gay consecration with church tradition and Scripture. I also wondered what her overall theological position was. I wanted to ask if she believed a person could be a Nicene Creed Christian and still support gay consecration. Is it possible, from her perspective, to have one foot in Jerusalem and the other in the Castro District?

St. Mark's Episcopal Church is located on the Boulevard, a long, wide street that cuts across the top of Richmond's Fan District—an eighty-square-block collection of row houses, apartments, restaurants, and bars (forty at current count), art students, professionals, and longtime residents. This is an area that very much belies Richmond's reputation as a thoroughly conservative city. A half-block to the north of the church, on Monument Avenue, is the Stonewall Jackson equestrian statue. St. Mark's was founded a few years after Jackson died from wounds inflicted by his own troops; he was a strict Calvinist, so perhaps to some degree he expected what was coming. The church's first rector is listed as the Rev. Thomas G. Deshal, who served from 1866 to 1892. The current church was built in the early 1900s. Membership is around four hundred, with far fewer than half attending the 10:00 A.M. Sunday services I visited. Many of the congregants were middle-aged and older, though the bulletin listed sixteen new confirmands along with eight reaffirmations. Rector Levy had come on board in 1997. She was said to be a powerful preacher.

I had some time before the St. Mark's service began and decided to drop in on a couple of neighborhood churches to see how other outposts of the mainline were fairing. A few miles up Monument Avenue I found the Episcopal Church of the Holy Comforter. A large wooden Decalogue hung in the antechamber, though inside the sanctuary few admonitions were delivered. The priest instead spoke of how he "felt the edge of the envelope everywhere" as the church "reached out to claim and bless all God's children." God is busy "expanding the circle" of the faithful. He quoted W. H. Auden and told several jokes, to good effect. Though the congregation was small in number, it clearly enjoyed his banter.

A few miles down Monument Avenue the Rev. Debbie Harris was the guest minister at St. John's United Church of Christ. St. John's is on Stuart Circle, named for Confederate hero J. E. B. Stuart, whose statue is not far from the church's front door. The Rev. Harris's audience numbered about two dozen. Most were older people. She nonetheless gave a spirited sermon, noting that in our day the "bottom line is everything," which, she added, was the way it was in Jesus's day as well. "Seven percent of the population controlled 90 percent of the wealth," she said; Jesus condemned the rich. She also said that God is "deeply inclusive" and busy "bringing about love and justice. The kingdom of God is happening now." It is vitally important, she concluded, to "push God's agenda in the world."

By the time I arrived at St. Mark's, the Rev. Levy had already ascended the pulpit. From my vantage point at the back of the church she appeared birdlike, but she spoke with a piercing voice. She invoked Gideon as if he were a close friend and adviser. She spoke with urgency about God's "power to work miracles." There was no indication that she believed the biblical miracles were fables. Nor was there a single mention of politics, directly or through the use of the code words—"inclusive," "pushing the envelope," etc.—heard in the other churches.

She turned to the Beatitudes and noted that these should not be taken as advice from Jesus but instead as his observations about the nature of life. "Woe to the rich," she said—but not because they control too much wealth. Jesus was simply pointing out that those who are rich today may find themselves poor tomorrow. Downtimes are part of life, she continued, and perhaps they are the most profitable of times for spiritual growth. She quoted Paul's view that "God uses weakness to shame the strong," then turned to Shakespeare's Lear, who fell far, she acknowledged, but in his madness may have seen deeper into the true nature of life than when he was confined by the "trappings of kingship." Then she was done. It was communion time. The choir sang the Nicene Creed as I made my exit.

I took with me a few church publications. One contained a reprint of gay parishioner Karen Hardison's support for creating rites for same-sex unions. "We baptize all who acknowledge what God has already done. We invite all those who are so baptized to the Table . . . again because God already does so." But the church, she continued, had drawn the line at blessing her relationship. "My rector is unable to preside over a celebration and blessing of what God has done and is doing in the life of Amy & myself. We have been together almost 14 years. We have been through the fires of hell & emerged stronger and more committed than we could have imagined. God willing we will one day have a child in our family. . . . We will baptize our baby in the church, we will make promises to our child. . . . We will tell her that she belongs to God's family in every way possible for always. . . . We will let her know that the church is home. . . . We do not want to have to warn that little child that all this will be true in the eyes of God forever, but in the eyes of the church only if she is not gay."

Sandra Levy introduced herself as Dr. Sandra Levy; her entry on the list of St. Mark's rectors (in the church antechamber) includes "PhD" after her name. When answering a call for an appointment, her assistant referred to her as the "very reverend" Sandra M. Levy. She is a woman who takes her doctorate and post seriously. She is very slender with thick silver hair, cut fairly close. I detected some wariness in her eyes; I suspected she had gotten a heads-up from Rector Gray, or that Google might have been to blame. She invited me into her small study, which was furnished with a desk, wing chair, and sofa, where she directed me to sit.

She quickly pointed out that she too is married. Before entering the priesthood, she had been an associate professor of psychiatry at the University of Pittsburgh. The doctorate, from Indiana University in Bloomington, is in clinical psychology. Her research specialty was psychoneuroimmunology and cancer risk, which she called a "sexy" area of expertise. She had been highly regarded, traveling many places to discuss her research, including Germany and Israel. She was also associate director of the Pittsburgh Cancer Institute at the university.

I asked about her religious credentials. She was raised a Catholic but had gone over to the Episcopal Church fifteen years ago. Why? "They would ordain me," she responded, eyes sparkling. The Rev. Levy, it seems, had undertaken an exodus of her own.

She graduated from the Virginia Theological Seminary in 1994 and came to St. Mark's in 1997. The church has a large gay membership, she said, probably 20 percent, though she does not consider the church to be militant on the Robinson consecration issue. She was certainly not militant, she added, and found biblical support for her position in Paul's Letter to the Galatians, where he writes, "We are all one in the Lord Jesus." I asked her the questions I had asked Rector Gray, and she echoed each talking point, including the Old Testament passage on stoning adulteresses. The spirit of the New Testament leads one away from condemning sexual practices that are part of committed relationships, she insisted. It is also her opinion, informed by her professional background, that most homosexuals "do not choose" their orientation. They are playing the hand life has dealt them. Her parishioners, gay and straight, seemed to accept that premise and were, with one or two exceptions, supportive of the Robinson consecration.

But she did not share Rector Gray's view of those who disagreed with her. There was no touch of wariness or condescension. She said she understood the distress traditionalists feel over what is happening in their church, though she believed that much of it has nothing to do with theology. "People don't handle sex very well," she said, sitting forward. "Homosexuality is an explosive, gut issue." Episcopalians had adapted to other changes that challenged tradition without threatening to leave the denomination, she reminded me, but not in an accusing way. Homosexuality is different. "I don't think it will be accommodated as easily as divorce and remarriage and women's ordination." Nonetheless, she considered the Robinson consecration "a big step forward" and assumed there will be, in many churches at least, a rite available that recognizes "the goodness of unions" that are outside of marriage. She understood the traditionalists' concern about calling such unions marriage. "I don't know that it will be called marriage," she said.

"Marriage is a legal relationship between a man and woman that holds the possibility of procreation." She is for a type of "goodness" blessing that would be apart from marriage and not challenge its status.

While the Rev. Levy was not interested in criticizing those within her denomination, she was not similarly restrained on the subject of Catholicism. "No self-respecting woman can be Catholic," she said. The refusal to ordain women placed Catholicism beyond the boundaries of reasonableness. This seemed a good time to bring up the Virgin Birth.

Did she believe in it?

The Virgin Birth, she responded after a moderate pause, was not a "biological mechanism" by which Jesus was introduced to the world. The larger story, she said, is that "God intervened in the world and did a great thing in history."

What about the Resurrection? True or false? It was strange asking a priest if she believed in the foundational belief of the Christian religion. But the Rev. Levy was quick and emphatic with her answer.

"There was a resurrection. There was some bodily integrity," not merely a "spiritual resurrection." Of that she was sure, though much else is mysterious and perhaps unknowable. "We grope to find the meaning of our faith. We won't know all these things until the veil is lifted."

As I was leaving, the Rev. Levy made an unexpected and refreshing admission. She was not sure how "all this will come out," which I took as an acknowledgment that perhaps gay consecration and the establishment of rites that will bless not only same-sex marriages but other relationships outside of marriage as well might do grievous damage to the denomination.

Candor may not be a biblical virtue, but it is a fairly rare earthly phenomenon, especially when contentious issues are the subject. Yet I wondered after leaving if the Rev. Levy is as adamant about the Resurrection in her pulpit as she had been in her office. As it happened, we were coming up on Easter, and so that morning I slipped into the back of St. Mark's for the early service. In her sermon the Rev. Levy assured her congregation that Jesus rose "just as surely as I stand before you this morning." Her tone was one of piercing certitude. She was equally strong in dismissing the notion that the Resurrection is Christianity's updating of the fertility myths. I have listened to many Easter sermons, none more passionately delivered.

At the same time, the Rev. Levy's sermon raised a powerful question: how can priests who so strongly believe the most unbelievable of their religion's teachings—that Jesus rose from the dead—simultaneously reject as unbelievable his admonitions against sexual relationships outside of marriage? Progressives portray this ability as the sign of a subtle and learned mind. Others of us might sense profound incoherence. In any event, the Rev. Levy did make clear that a visitor can enter a politically liberal Episcopal church and hear it preached that Christ was crucified, buried, and risen. Something for everyone, under one roof. By economic measures, this would be a recipe for success.

Yet it is failing.

I was now on my way to northern Virginia to visit the rebellious Episcopalians. When leaving St. John's, I told Rector Gray that my first stop would be to visit Hugo Blankingship Jr., a lawyer who has played a central role in the Walter Righter heresy trial (brought because Righter had ordained a gay deacon) and who was now deeply involved in establishing the network of breakaway churches.

"Oh, yes," Rector Gray replied. He was quite familiar with

Hugo Blankingship Jr. In fact, he said, "his father is buried here in the churchyard."

Rector Gray walked me out among the gravestones. Edgar Allan Poe's mother, Elizabeth Arnold Poe, 1787–1811, is buried near the east fence. Elsewhere are the graves of revolutionary figures, including George Wythe, 1726–1805, whose tombstone remembers him as "Teacher of Randolph, Jefferson, and Marshall" and "First Virginia signer of the Declaration of Independence." Along another row is the grave of a stonecutter and bricklayer named Abraham Shield, who died at age twenty-eight in 1798, and Bessie M. Sims, 1895–1972, a "Missionary to China." Just to the left of her grave is the tombstone for Alexander Hugo Blankingship, 1894–1975, "Third Bishop of Cuba."

"I wonder what the old bishop might be thinking about developments in his church," I said.

"He lived in a different time," Rector Gray responded.

Two

The Departing Episcopalians

In the Name of Tradition

After talking with Rector Gray and reading his colleagues' considered opinions, I found myself readjusting my view of clerics who cannot seem to live by the demands of their faith, as delineated in their holy texts, but do not break free and walk on their own. My prior view was that such people deserve sympathy: they seem not to have the intellectual power to make a break and so are stuck in a no-man's-land between the secular and religious worlds, fully enjoying neither. I assumed there must be, at a deep level, a sense of profound failure—a sense that they are in the grip of a neurosis they cannot escape.

It was now dawning on me that a different dynamic is at work. These clerics are doing missionary work, though not of the sort one would immediately imagine. They have considered God's ways, as revealed in their faith's Scriptures and traditions, and have found them wanting. Indeed, they may consider them little more than the scratchings of crazed desert nomads suffering from a combination of dehydration, dementia, and delusions of grandeur. They have a higher agenda to advance, one that promises to improve upon a failed understanding of God's will, or in some instances to improve upon the will of a failed God. This allows them to turn Holy Writ on its head: what was once forbidden becomes acceptable, if not celebrated; admonitions toward holy living suddenly become hate speech.

The Baptists we visit with in chapter 6 have a word for all this: pride, and perhaps diabolical pride at that. There's another word for all this: victory. The progressive forces have ousted their traditionalist pewmates and taken over their denomination, albeit a denomination that is shrinking toward oblivion. Which brings up my position: the progressive clerics are talking themselves out of a job. Their admonitions that we should all be nice to one another—be accepting, tolerant, hospitable, and open—are welcome enough in a harsh world. Yet they are not giving the world anything it cannot get from television chat shows, movies, op-ed pieces, and the other soapboxes where contemporary sages gather. Their advice is much the same, if not identical, and sofas are much more comfortable than pews.

Or so I mused on my way to see Hugo Blankingship Jr., son of the Rt. Rev. Hugo Blankingship, Bishop of Cuba, interred in St. John's churchyard—now enemy territory of sorts. Hugo Blankingship Jr. is a successful lawyer with offices in Fairfax County, Virginia, one of the nation's richest counties and home to several churches central to the breakaway movement. He has been back and forth to see the Archbishop of Canterbury over the past few years and was presenter of the conservative position in the Walter Righter heresy trial, reasonably known as the Traditionalists' Last Stand. He is also married to my father's cousin.

I had begun our conversation (held in his expansive law offices) by mentioning that Rector Gray and I had stood at his father's grave a week previously and wondered aloud how the bishop might be reacting to current events within his church.

"He's spinning in his grave," Hugo instantly responded. And the bishop was not one to spin without serious provocation. Hugo Sr. had become a bishop in 1939 and by our standards was something of a rare bird: an Episcopal evangelist. He took the Christian message of hope to the island, teaching that even those with the most limited of prospects should see their lives in a great context— as part of a much larger drama that began in antiquity and would extend past the end of time. The island's poor field hands were themselves the children of God, their salvation purchased with the blood of the Son of Man. That was the bishop's message. Then along came Fidel Castro. Bishop Blankingship's days were numbered. He left the country a few weeks after the Bay of Pigs, "under duress," Hugo Jr. recalled with a wry smile.

On his return to the states, Hugo Jr. continued, the bishop discovered that another revolution was under way: "Theological liberalism was taking over the seminaries." The Episcopal Church had long been friendly to liberal causes, to be sure. Its pacifist wing fluttered as World War II loomed; the church declared that armed combat was "incompatible with the teaching and example of our Lord Jesus Christ," a belief echoed in our day by Presiding Bishop Frank Griswold and the church's Executive Council, who denounced intervention in Iraq as "an unacceptable form of action for Christians who are called by Christ to be peacemakers." Theological liberalism, by some accounts, had begun early in the last century, but when the bishop came home, every element of the Creed was up for negotiation and none survived intact, including the Resurrection. So far as some of the clergy were concerned, and there were bishops numbered among them, Jesus had died on that bloody cross and rotted in the ground. Many who did not go so far as to adopt that position strongly supported the right to dissent by those who did. The heretic had become a hero.

Hugo Blankingship and his fellow traditionalists had been on the defensive for decades, and with the Robinson consecration they began eyeing the exits. They were busy organizing a network of dissenting churches and had called on conservative bishops from the Anglican Communion to provide oversight. The Anglican Communion, of which the Episcopal Church is a small branch, had not been immune to similar controversy. Just before our meeting, the Rt. Rev. Michael Ingham, Anglican bishop of the diocese of New Westminster, had shut down a small Vancouver church for opposing gay unions. Bishop Ingham was not happy that traditionalist churches in his care had withheld around $375,000 (in U.S. dollars) because of his decision to bless such unions. He had earlier filed ecclesiastical charges against seven dissenting parishes in the diocese for disobedience and "scandalous conduct." Similar acts of ostracism were occurring around the United States, all of which, Hugo Jr. said, was much more serious than when conservative Episcopalians had asked the pro-Robinson Bishop Lee to stay away from their church—a story that was covered by the *New York Times:* "We would respectfully ask that, instead of you visiting All Saints' on Nov. 9, 2003, you send Bishop Gray for confirmation," an All Saints' member had told the bishop. "Our people are so distressed by your views that contradict the very clear teaching of Scripture that your visit this fall would be painful and divisive."

"Gasps arose from the crowd," the *Times* noted.

Blankingship shook his head. "That's not much compared to having your church shut down."

I had two primary questions for Hugo Blankingship Jr. Why had they drawn the line at the consecration of Gene Robinson? After all, there have been far more serious theological provocations, including bishops who rejected the core beliefs of Christianity. The second question was more expansive: How did the traditionalists lose their denomination? Why were they unable to resist the progressive advance?

Blankingship was quick to insist that the formation of the breakaway church network was "not about homosexuality" but about authority. Bishops around the country should not be allowed to amend or, as it happens, ignore church teachings as they choose, he said. That results in theological chaos, and chaos is already much advanced, perhaps to the terminal stages. Traditionalists have been leaving the denomination for decades, some of them starting schismatic churches.

He and his traditionalist colleagues, he continued, have done all that is possible to defend church traditions. They have even taken the extraordinary step of bringing a renegade bishop up on heresy charges. That bishop was Walter Righter. Hugo Blankingship presented the accusers' position.

Blankingship and his fellow accusers thought they had the better argument. They had Holy Scripture, Episcopal tradition, and indeed the full sway of Christian teaching on their side. Their paperwork was very much in order. As they were to find, tradition and Scripture no longer carry much weight in the Episcopal Church.

The Walter Righter trial was held in Wilmington, Delaware, in May 1996. Righter had six years previously ordained a man named Barry Stopfel as a deacon. Stopfel, who was later ordained a priest, was involved in a gay relationship. All was fairly calm for five years, but then ten bishops filed charges against Righter. The charge: he had broken faith with church teachings. This was no small matter, the accusers insisted. False doctrine finds harsh appraisal in the New Testament. It is said to be a means by which the Devil attacks the Bride of Christ. If individual bishops could institute a change of this magnitude and get away with it, bishops anywhere could teach anything they wanted. The denomination would fall into total incoherence—a path down which it had already perilously advanced.

Blankingship and his colleagues believed they had several strong cards to play. The first was doctrine.

"What is doctrine?" their argument began (the following quotations are taken from court documents). "Does the Episcopal

Church have any doctrine? Are standards of moral conduct a matter of doctrine in this Church? Around these questions centers the issue now before the Court. The Constitution and Prayer Book require allegiance to Church doctrine. A bishop may not teach contrary to that doctrine."

The Rt. Rev. Righter, the accusers insisted, had acted as a free agent. His clear mission had been to "affect the criteria of future ordinations" by ordaining a homosexual, "thereby teaching a doctrine not held by this Church." There could be no doubt that gay ordination was a violation of doctrine. "From apostolic times, the Church has recognized a 'rule of faith' inherent in the biblical Gospel, which later was formulated in the creeds. This principle of a summary of normative teaching also applied in the area of morality and sexual morality in particular. Thus the earliest, subapostolic writing, the Diadache, or Teaching of the Twelve Apostles, begins by delineating 'two ways, one of life and one of death,' and immediately turns to sexual moral teaching against adultery, pederasty, and fornication."

Such was their basic argument from doctrine. Their next witness was Scripture, starting with the Old Testament, in which homosexuality "is condemned in the moral law of Moses as an 'abomination,' an offense both to the holiness of God and to his created order." The New Testament built upon the Old. "Jesus incorporates most of the Old Testament teaching about sexuality," they argued. Indeed, "Jesus' sexual ethic is more strenuous than the Old Testament's. He refers to the creation stories in affirming marriage and identifies exclusive monogamy as the primal purpose of God and exclusive celibacy as a sign of discipleship. For Jesus and the Christian Church thereafter Genesis creation stories were normative references for teaching about human sexual relations." Saint Paul, they added, was of identical mind. "In addressing the Corinthians, he writes: 'Do you not know . . . that neither fornicators, nor idolaters, nor adulterers, nor homosexuals will inherit the kingdom of God? And such were some of you. But you were washed, you were sanctified, you were justified in the name of the Lord Jesus Christ and in the Spirit of our God.'"

This final passage, it should be noted, is at the center of the disagreement between progressives and traditionalists on the nature of homosexuality. We shall see it again when we visit the Southern Baptists, who base their understanding of homosexuality, and especially their belief that homosexuality can be "cured" through the intervention of the Holy Spirit, on these few sentences. Paul also denounced homosexuality in his letter to the Romans, warning of "disordered desires in which their women exchanged natural relations for unnatural, and the men likewise gave up natural relations with women and were consumed with passion for one another, men committing shameless acts with men."

The accusers had invoked church doctrine and both Testaments of the Bible. They had made the argument that there is such a thing as sin and that by any reasonable reading of Scripture homosexual behavior is sinful. Sin, they felt required to remind the court, is recognized by their church as something much to be avoided, and their church had gone on record many times about the sin at the heart of this dispute.

The bishops of the Church of England, for instance, had agreed that "sexual activity of any kind outside marriage comes to be seen as sinful, and homosexual practice as especially dishonorable." There is "relatively little mention of homosexuality in Patristic literature because there was no debate on the subject," they added. Thomas Aquinas himself "elaborated the Biblical and patristic understanding of homosexuality as being 'against nature' for humans, both in their capacity as animals and as rational beings." In more recent history the bishops had in 1930 condemned "illicit and irregular unions" as being "contrary to the revealed will of God," and in a 1987 resolution they declared that "sexual intercourse is an act of total commitment which belongs properly within a permanent marriage relationship; that fornication and adultery are sins against this ideal, and are to be met by a call to repentance and the exercise of compassion; that homosexual acts also fall short of this ideal, and are likewise to be met by a call to repentance and the exercise of compassion." In 1991 the bishops restated the position once more: "Homophile orientation and its expression in sexual activity do not constitute a parallel and alternative form of human sexuality as complete within the terms of the created order as the heterosexual. The convergence of Scripture, tradition and reasoned reflection on experience, even including the newly sympathetic and perceptive thinking of our own day, makes it impossible for the Church to come with integrity to any other conclusion."

Doctrine, Scripture, and all of Christian history were on their side, the accusers believed. They had all their paperwork in order. They had made a powerful case. Now they were to find that their paper case was very much beside the point.

Bishop Frederick Borsch of Los Angeles reminded the court that "Scripture clearly says remarriage is adultery, so there seems to be a strong reinterpretation of those Scriptures" in the earlier approval of remarriage after divorce. Clearly, Borsch said, the church had changed its position, and did that not also constitute a change in doctrine? Did the accusers wish to argue that this change is supported by Scripture? It was of course true that the Episcopal Church had gone on record several times in opposition to homosexuality. It had done the same regarding divorce and remarriage and the ordination of females.

Why, the court was left to ponder, were the accusers drawing the line at this particular issue?

The church officials involved in the trial, Blankingship told me, conducted themselves in a civil manner, even though, he added, it was assumed that a meaningful proportion had personal reasons for supporting gay ordination. But Blankingship and his colleagues came under withering fire from other quarters.

Gay activist (and Episcopalian) Louie Crew crafted a scathing and widely distributed attack on the conservative position entitled "Is There a Heretic in the House?" This trial was not about doctrine, Scripture, or mere tradition, Crew argued. It was an attempt to scapegoat gays and lesbians. "Scapegoating is evil," Crew wrote. If one were looking for immorality, the conservatives held all those cards. In addition, the Episcopal Church was making "a public spectacle of itself." It had become a laughingstock. This heresy trial was the "high church" version of the Scopes trial, in which Blankingship and company were using an "antiquated notion of God" to "deprive God's people of the right to use their minds and hearts to attend to new truth." This was very bad form, which is a high sin with Episcopalians. Then Crew made an especially invidious comparison: "In backing the state and William Jennings Bryan in 1925, parts of the church wrote themselves out of the lives of many of the best minds in America. . . . Every Episcopalian with half an IQ point left ought to be profoundly embarrassed. The vast majority of adult Episcopalians fled denominations where they had to hang their minds at the door, and now we are captive to a trial where such mindlessness is aired for all the world to see."

Crew's brilliant polemic was not only a rejection of doctrine, Scripture, and tradition, at least as the traditionalists viewed that trinity. It perfectly captured the spirit of the age, an age that had passed Blankingship and his colleagues by. Their world had been turned upside down. That which they believed most important— fidelity to doctrine and God's Word—was now considered an expression of hatred. That which they believed to be the eternal Truth was now dismissed as ignorance. The traditionalists had become strangers in their own house, and unwelcome strangers at that.

The decision went against the accusers. As the Episcopal News Service summarized, "The court held that neither the doctrine nor the discipline of the church currently prohibit the ordination of a non-celibate homosexual person living in a committed relationship." The majority opinion added that the court "is not giving an opinion on the morality of same gender relationships. We are not deciding whether life-long, committed, sexual same gender relationships are or are not a wholesome example with respect to ordination vows. We are not rendering an opinion on whether a bishop and diocese should or should not ordain persons living in same sex relationships. Rather, we are deciding the narrow issue of whether or not under Title IV [the church's disciplinary canons] a bishop is restrained from ordaining persons living in a committed same gender sexual relationship."

But everyone watching knew what the decision meant. Gay ordination had been given the green light. And if a gay priest is acceptable, why not a gay bishop? The line was thus drawn straight from Delaware to Minneapolis. And if Louie Crew is correct about 20 percent of priests being homosexual, this will be a road much traveled. For many traditionalists, the green light had also been given: it was time to clear out.

On July 22–25, 2003, just before Gene Robinson's elevation, conservative Episcopalians met at Truro Church in Fairfax. They had by now seen the writing on the wall and drawn up their farewell addresses. "We are mainstream Anglican leaders from Provinces around the world comprising a majority of the world's 75 million Anglicans," they stated in a declaration. "We have gathered on the eve of the General Convention of the Episcopal Church out of profound love for the church and a deep concern for the constitutional crisis that confronts us. The proposed actions by the General Convention to confirm a non-celibate homosexual as a bishop of this Communion or to approve the creation of liturgies for the blessing of relationships outside of marriage would shatter the church."

They expected the shattering to occur and announced what their response would be. The "proposed actions will precipitate a dramatic realignment of the Church. The American bishops at this meeting have prayed, planned and are prepared to respond as faithful members of the Anglican Communion. Should these events occur, the majority of the Primates anticipate convening an extraordinary meeting at which they too will respond to the actions of General Convention." Signatories to the declaration included Peter Akinola, archbishop of Nigeria; Drexel Gomez, archbishop of the West Indies; Emmanuel Kolini, archbishop of Rwanda; Bernard Malango, archbishop of Central Africa; and Yong Ping Chung, archbishop of Southeast Asia. These are the bishops Rector Gray warns are being funded by a secretive billionaire with theocratic visions.

The decision to create a network of dissenting churches overseen by African bishops is probably not nearly as nefarious as the rector would have us believe. But it does underscore the fact that what is known as the premier brand name in mainline Protestantism is shattering, which may be a preview of events to come across the mainline. And calling in the African Anglicans also underscores how much the world has been turned on its head: by calling in the African Anglicans, the traditionalists are reversing history, which takes us back to where this chapter began, St. John's Church.

Patrick Henry's "liberty or death" speech targeted the British, but Henry had sharpened his rhetorical teeth on the Anglican Church, which was established at the founding of the Virginia colony (1607) and operated as a near-monopoly. The government built Anglican churches and paid Anglican priests. Rivals were required to petition for permission to so much as preach a sermon. Missing church was punishable by fine.

A growing number of Virginians found this to be not only oppressive but spiritually substandard to the alternative offered by roving evangelicals such as British Methodist George Whitfield, who in 1739 visited Williamsburg to great sensation. His sermons became the focus of worship meetings held in private residences—early America's version of the "home church." By 1743 there were four "reading houses" outside Richmond, including one named after land grant recipient George Polegreen, where Scripture readings, sermonizing, and hymn singing ("Lord, I Want to Be a Christian in My Heart" was believed to have premiered at Polegreen) found an expanding audience.

Among Polegreen's devoted visitors were Patrick Henry and his mother. This put them in a somewhat uncomfortable position, according to Jan Swearingen, a professor at Texas A&M University. The presiding Anglican priest was Henry's paternal uncle and namesake, Patrick Henry Sr. Nonetheless, young Patrick soon fell under the spell of Samuel Davies, a Presbyterian minister at Polegreen and the first non-Anglican to preach legally in Virginia. Reading Davies (thanks to excerpts provided by Professor Swearingen), one understands immediately why Henry later cited him as a primary rhetorical influence. In a sermon supporting the French and Indian War, Davies promised that "Jesus, the Prophet of Galilee, will push his conquests from country to country until all nations submit to him. . . . Has he not rooted out the enmity of your carnal minds, and sweetly constrained you to the most affectionate obedience? Make this country a dutiful province of the dominion of Thy grace. My brethren, should we all become his willing subjects, he would not longer suffer the perfidious slaves of France, and their savage allies, to chastise and punish us for our rebellion against him; but peace shall again run down like a river and righteousness like a mighty stream."

Henry's first major rhetorical target was the Anglican clergy; his "parson's cause" speech, delivered in 1763, included these thunderbolts: "We have heard a great deal about the benevolence and holy zeal of our reverend clergy, but how is this manifested? Do they manifest their zeal in the cause of religion and humanities, by practicing the mild and benevolent precepts of the Gospel of Jesus? Do they feed the hungry and clothe the naked? Oh no, gentlemen! Instead of feeding the hungry and clothing the naked, these rapacious harpies would, were their powers equal to their will, snatch from the hearth of their honest parishioner his last hoe cake, from the widow and her orphan children their last milk cow, the last bed, nay, the last blanket from the lying-in woman!" This speech, according to Swearingen, marked "the beginning of the end of rigid Anglican rule over religious life in Virginia."

Two hundred forty years later, Episcopal traditionalists seek a reassertion of Anglican influence. Like Bishop Blankingship, Henry is reasonably assumed to be spinning in his grave, perhaps in several directions. One assumes he would be on the side of the traditionalists on the consecration issue. "They consecrated a *what?*" would be his likely response to the news from Minneapolis. Yet he would also be horrified that his theological kinsmen had turned to his old nemesis—the Anglicans. That the rescuers would be mostly black African bishops would inspire total discombobulation.

As their exodus from the Episcopal Church gained momentum, the tone of some departing dissidents' farewells became somewhat Henryesque. Diane Knippers, a Washington, D.C.– based conservative intellectual, addressed a meeting of the American Anglican Council (AAC) in Dallas on October 8, 2003, and assured her audience that "I will not be advocating riots in the streets, one response of the faithful in fifth-century Constantinople." She had, however, "thought about a demonstration around the National Cathedral, but not riots." As a longtime warrior in the culture wars, Knippers knew that the first order of spin is to claim victory. "The first thing I want to emphasize is that we are the church. One thing of which we laity must repent is our tendency to be cowed by clericalism. Of course we respect our godly leaders, and of course we respect the offices and roles of bishops and priests. But the model that Scripture gives us for the Church of Jesus Christ is not a corporate flow chart or a military chain of command. It is a body. All the members are necessary, all play a role, all are to be honored. And let's face it, we are a very big part of the body."

The American Anglican Council, she said, would take its cues from the fifth-century monk Vincent of Lerins, who held that "authentic Christian doctrine and teaching is that which has been believed everywhere, always, by everyone." Scripture would continue to be their guide, and tradition would guard Scripture. Innovation would be allowed, but only so long as it was Scripturally based. "Will the actions of the 2003 General Convention be understood as a part of the general consensus of the Christian faith? The laity have a responsibility to say *no*. We will not receive this innovation." She also reminded her audience that many Christians had died defending orthodoxy. It had not yet come to that, yet. But some churches had already begun the act of disassociation. Who knew where this road would lead? She invoked Martin Luther's "A Mighty Fortress Is Our God" to shore up flagging spirits:

> *Let goods and kindred go, this mortal life also;*
> *The body they may kill: God's truth abideth still,*
> *His kingdom is forever.*

The dissidents were not without their supporters, though support tended to come from abroad. From Uganda, the second-

largest Anglican community in Africa (after Nigeria), church officials sent word that they had severed ties with the Episcopal
Church because of the Robinson consecration; its spokesman said
that "any same sex relationship is a disorder of God's creation."
This would hurt the Ugandans' cash flow. They now considered
any money from an Episcopal church to be tainted and would accept no more donations. Bishops claiming to represent 50 million
Anglicans announced they were in a "state of impaired communion" with the Episcopal Church. The Russian Orthodox Church
sent word from Moscow that it "cannot condone the perversion of
human nature" and so would be cutting ties with the Episcopal
Church. The Network of Anglican Communion Dioceses and
Parishes named a moderator (Bishop Robert Duncan of Pittsburgh) and posted its theological statement, which said that the
pro-consecration liberals had "torn the fabric of the Anglican
Communion." The network therefore had no choice but to
"oppose assaults on the authority of the Scriptures. We are also
called to oppose assaults on the way of life that the Scriptures en-
join (1 Tim. 6:3–6). This opposition comes, not from a divisive
spirit, but from the precious vocation to holiness, which leads us
away from sin into the clear and obedient participation in God's
own nature."

Hugo Blankingship ended our conversation by expressing the
hope that one day this upheaval will be seen as a "new reformation" within the church. But another analysis, widely circulated by
conservatives, holds out no such hope. It also offers a convincing
answer to my other question: why were the traditionalists unable
to thwart the progressive advance?

Its author, Philip Turner, was born into a family that has
claimed membership in the Episcopal Church "as far back as any-

one can remember." Much of his career has been spent teaching in Episcopal seminaries. His title tells the story: "The End of a Church and the Triumph of Denominationalism." While the essay was written about the Episcopal Church USA, with slight emendations it could be used to describe the unraveling of other denominations within the mainline.

Many contemporary Episcopalians, Turner begins, "were not all too fond of identifying themselves with a faith which had settled the major and most minor points of human existence many centuries previous. That was not only dusty but reeked deeply of certitude, which they were quite certain was a very bad thing. And so a new self-image began to emerge reflecting this new certitude, one that was quick to embrace ideas that, for all extents and purposes, negated much of what the church had always stood for."

The loss of faith in the faith resulted in a loss of faith in authority, he continues. Bishop James Pike's contention that the "Church's classical way of stating what is represented by the doctrine of the Trinity is . . . not essential to the Christian faith" brought no disciplinary action. Pike was merely told to "consider himself censured." He was hailed as a hero by some bishops, Turner adds, and this incident made it clear that church fathers feared bad publicity far more than the wrath of God.

Female ordination was another sign of authority's weakening hold. In 1974 three bishops ordained eleven women as priests, despite the fact that two years earlier resolutions calling for female ordination had been rejected—twice. The rationale: it was "prophetic" to ordain women as a form of "protest against oppression and an act of solidarity with those who are oppressed—in this case women." Again, Turner notes, there was no meaningful discipline. To no one's surprise, in 1975 four more women were ordained, and while there was an uproar, the church "acceded to its legitimacy by failing to take effective disciplinary action."

There was no turning back. The denomination had become an engine of "enlightened culture and progressive cultural trends" whose bishops could advance "prophetic causes" without fear of significant disciplinary action. Two years later a lesbian was ordained a priest in New York by Bishop Paul Moore, who was lightly scolded. When the General Convention met in 1979, it declared that it was "not appropriate for this Church to ordain a practicing homosexual or any person who is engaged in heterosexual relations outside marriage." But the ordinations continued; these too, says Turner, were considered a "justice issue." After Hugo Blankingship Jr. came home a loser from the Righter trial, "the way was open for Bishops to ordain sexually active homosexual persons if they so chose. It was clear that no disciplinary consequences would follow."

The Episcopal Church that Philip Turner and Hugo Blankingship loved, as their fathers loved it, is gone. And while Turner agrees that the church is under heavy bombardment from without, he finds the fatal flaw within. "To think well about what is happening in ECUSA one must ask why the sirens of modernity have sung so sweetly in ECUSA's ears. My belief is that a religious rather than historical or sociological answer must, in the end, be given to this question." He quotes English theologian P. T. Forsythe—"If within us we have nothing above us we soon succumb to what is around us"—and then concludes that his church has become empty at the core. That vacuity is reflected in "the theology that currently dominates ECUSA's pulpits. The standard sermon in outline runs something like this: 'God is love, God's love is inclusive, God acts in justice to see that everyone is included, we therefore ought to be co-actors and co-creators with God to make the world over in the way he wishes.'"

———

The Episcopal Church's decline can be seen as an illustration of Dean Kelley's warning: churches that abandon traditional faith and take up worldly causes, however laudable they may seem, are likely to embrace severe decline, if not extinction. There is not much left of the church now: by one accounting, there are nearly twice as many lesbians in the United States as Episcopalians (1.5 percent of the population, as opposed to 0.78 percent). And while the Anglican Church is strong in Africa, it is severely weakened in places where it once held sway. The *Hindustan Times* reported in January 2003 that more people were attending mosques each week in Britain than the Church of England (930,000 Muslims as opposed to 916,000 Anglicans). Many corpses spin in the Old Country as well.

The Episcopal Church's descent toward subatomic status has been long, but it has not been lonely, as we shall see in the next chapter. Nor has the attack on traditionalism been subtle or without resonance. It has found support not only throughout the mainline but also among vast numbers of believers throughout the United States, many of whom are often assumed to be orthodox if not fundamentalist in their beliefs.

There have been unintended consequences as well. While progressive clerics made headlines, they also created many Catholic, Orthodox, and evangelical believers. There is much to separate these refugees, some of whose stories will make up the remaining chapters, but all are likely to agree with the Easter 2004 sermon given at Truro Church in Fairfax by the Rev. Martyn Minns, a high-profile member of the AAC. His message was once common in mainline churches. It now marks him as a dissident:

> God will not be mocked if we declare what God calls sin to be not sin.
>
> God will not be mocked even if we claim that God's Word is no longer relevant to the complexities of modern life.

God will not be mocked by a church that believes that it can change foundational truth by a majority vote.

God will not be mocked even if we do seem to be getting away with it for a while.

God will have the final word!

Three

Celebrity Heretics and Their Influence

The Wee Deity

Episcopalians aren't the only traditionalists fleeing the mainline. The Presbyterian Church USA has driven many former members into the religious marketplace, or perhaps deeper into the arms of their caddies. Some Presbyterians left behind acrid farewell notes. The Presbyterian Lay Committee shook the mainline church's dust from its feet in an October 2003 declaration: "We have prayerfully considered what God is saying to us in the midst of this crisis. With sorrow, we have concluded that spiritual schism exists within the Presbyterian Church (USA) because of a deep and irreconcilable disunion among its members over the person and work of Jesus Christ, the authority of God's Word written, and God's call to a holy life. We are two faiths within one denomination." These dissidents invoked the Episcopalian experience: "Our denomination hovers on the brink of a comparable catastrophe. The Covenant Network already has announced that it will seek the repeal of the definitive interpretation of our ordination standards at the 2004 General Assembly and that it will support a full-scale assault on those standards at the 2006 General Assembly."

The post-mainline diaspora thus gained another member (the Lay Committee is headquartered in Lenoir, North Carolina), and the Presbyterian Church USA gained yet more pew space, with which it was already well endowed. The United Methodist Church continues in its own sex wars, with some conservatives calling for formal division. It is a mistake, however, to assume that these upheavals, to use an expression from the Clinton years, are "all about sex." It is also incorrect to assume, as Philip Turner points out in his elegant elegy, that these changes are of entirely recent vintage. And as we shall see, it is a huge error to believe that orthodox Christianity has been diminished only in the progressive churches. Theological heterodoxy, oddity, inconsistency, and outright incoherence are common even in churches that are assumed to be safe havens of orthodoxy and among believers who are thought to subscribe to the "Bible says it, I believe it, that settles it" school. The man in the "born-again" T-shirt is often not the person he is thought to be.

While contemporary headlines focus on what are largely sexual disputes within the denominations, looking back a few decades we see that the chroniclers of mainline decline have also found other, much larger problems confronting their churches. By some estimates, the whole of Western civilization has been under attack, and church decline is simply part of a larger story. Some of these writers, little known outside their immediate circles and largely forgotten today, also wrote in a voice pleasantly devoid of the harangue factor common in our time, despite the seriousness of their subject and, in some cases, despite the desperate times in which they wrote.

Dr. John Baillie, for example, taught at Union Theological Seminary in New York and was also moderator of the Church of Scotland. In 1945 he published a thin work, *What Is Christian Civilization?* that was notable for its elegant grimness. The family—"the primary unit of the Christian common life and the primary agency for the transmission of the Christian heritage"—was under fierce pressure from a "social pattern which tends to the disintegration of the family and allows less and less opportunity for privacy and solitude, while at the same time frequently turning the next-door neighbor into a complete stranger." Equally destructive, Dr. Baillie believed, was "an industrial system which deprives the worker alike of the joy of labour and of any real sense of its dignity, cutting him off from nature in acquainting him only with a machine."

These processes were far advanced, he feared, and dark forces seemed to loom. "For I take it as certain that if Christian ideas do not regain something of their former hold upon our national life, we shall sooner or later fall victim to such pagan ideas as have lately been resuscitated in Germany—and not in Germany alone. If the Spirit of Christ departs from the homes of the people, they will not long be found 'empty and swept and garnished,' as so many of them are now, but evil spirits will enter in and either the old idols will be set up again or new ones fashioned." Dr. Baillie, bless him, found little reason for hope. "In proportion as a society relaxes its hold upon the eternal, it ensures the corruption of the temporal. All earthly civilizations are corruptible and must one day perish, the pax Britannica no less than the pax Romana, and Christendom no less than Babylon and Troy. But if most have perished prematurely, it was largely as victims of their own proud illusions."

Dr. Baillie would not have been much surprised by the meanderings, a few decades later, of an Episcopal priest named William V. Rauscher, rector of the Church of the Incarnation in New York. Rector Rauscher's *Church in Frenzy* (1980) offers a more entertaining snapshot of demise and includes some of the disputes that dominate our time. By the early 1960s, he believed, the church was "dangerously near what pilots call 'the point of no return.'" Telltale signs were all around. A clergyman in Falkenstein, East Germany, had become so distraught by "the existence of insurmountable differences in the field of religion and the shaping of the Christian way of life" that he "ignited himself from the altar candles and burst into a human inferno before three hundred hor-rified parishioners." Some clergymen were already conducting gay marriages "in which the phrase 'so long as you both shall love' pro-vides the proper escape clause." Abortion had gained substantial support—four years before the Supreme Court gave its nod—to the point that an English bishop had attempted to get an "abortion prayer" in the new prayer book: "Heavenly Father, you are the Giver of Life and you share with us the care of the life that is given. Into your hands we commit in trust the developing life that we have cut short. Look in kindly judgment on the decision that we have made and assure us in all our uncertainty that your love for us can never change. Amen."

Divorce and remarriage were taking their toll. "People who are sincere are not encouraged by the church when they read that Rex Harrison, who was married six times and divorced five times (a wife died) and married for the seventh time, received the blessing of the church at the Little Church Around the Corner in New York City. . . . Nor is it helpful to local churches when they deal with such aftereffects as the seventh marriage of Elizabeth Taylor Hilton Wilding Todd Fisher Burton Warner by an Episcopal rec-tor in Middleburg, Virginia. Is such a wedding 'signifying unto us the mystical union that is betwixt Christ and his Church . . . and therefore not to be entered into inadvisedly or lightly?'" Even proper weddings had taken on a Las Vegas air. Brides might re-quest songs such as "Indian Love Call" or "How Do You Solve a Problem Like Maria?" he complained, and ceremonies "can con-tain anything from a reading of Gibran to a poem by Timothy Leary." Jimmy Durante "was buried from the Roman Catholic church while the organist played 'Inka Dinka Doo' and 'Give My Regards to Broadway.'" Easter services had been trivialized and Palm Sunday parades were now advertised as "fun." Ash Wednes-day had in some places lost its solemn edge. In one Maryland church, "the ashes applied to the foreheads of about a hundred men and women consisted of human blood, olive oil, tax forms, and a draft card. A slight variation from the usual burning of blessed palms of the previous Lent." Elsewhere, "pietistic pastors" were authenticating bleeding statues and blessing tortillas, the Rev. Rauscher noted with genial exasperation. "In March 1977, following the death of a Canadian priest named Cyrille Labreque, mourners noticed the image of Christ on the sole of his shoe. Soon some fifty thousand people had flocked to see the image on the leather sole when the toe was pointed downward." What's next? he wondered. "Will someone see His face in an ice cube floating in a vodka tonic?"

One imagines these old priests sitting in their studies, thinking of a time when a magisterial liturgy shared the room with Bach and Scarlatti. Now Timothy Leary danced to "Inka Dinka Doo." The old church fathers were surely spinning in their graves.

The deeper problem, however, was that some clergymen, including bishops, were saying that Jesus might be spinning in his as well. It was their belief that Jesus had been swallowed up by the earth just as surely as had Pilate and Judas, and for that matter Caligula and Stalin. He was crucified, dead, buried, and rotted. This was taught from Christian pulpits.

Among other things, that was not a church-sustaining belief, even when it was simultaneously insisted that Jesus was a first-rate philosopher and aesthete and otherwise well worth emulation. As a pile of dust, Jesus simply has little drawing power; his church no longer gives the world something only the church can give—a religion based on the life and teachings of the One said to be the "firstborn of the dead." Nor was it necessary for a sizable portion of the clergy to suggest such a belief. A denomination that allowed even a few priests or bishops to maintain their position after disavowing the Resurrection, as Philip Turner points out, had ceded authority and, by allowing the celebrity heretics to keep their jobs, offered an endorsement of sorts. This not only destroyed a sense of theological coherence. It suggested that the church could be for and against its core belief, simultaneously. This sort of "tolerance" would not be likely in the world of business: a company dedicated to racial tolerance and advancement would not be expected to keep on board a vice president who suddenly announced that blacks were inferior beings. That Episcopal Bishop John Shelby Spong, now retired (as of 2000), was allowed to stay on suggests at least a fair degree of sympathy in high places for his skepticism.

Because contemporary headlines have been obsessed with sexual issues, especially homosexuality, it is easy to forget the extent to which some clergymen rejected core Christian teachings and as a result forced traditional believers into exile. Here is a statement of beliefs publicly distributed by one of the more high-profile celebrity heretics:

- "I do not define God as a supernatural being."

- "I cannot interpret Jesus as the earthly incarnation of this supernatural deity."

- "I do not believe that this Jesus could or did in any literal way raise the dead, overcome a medically diagnosed paralysis, or restore sight to a person born blind or to one in whom the ability to see had been physiologically destroyed."

- "I do not believe Jesus entered this world by the miracle of a virgin birth or that virgin births occur anywhere except in mythology."

- "I do not believe that the experience Christians celebrate at Easter was the physical resurrection of the three-day-dead body of Jesus, nor do I believe that anyone literally talked with Jesus after the resurrection moment, gave him food, touched his resurrected flesh, or walked in any physical manner with his risen body."

- "I do not believe that Jesus, at the end of this earthly sojourn, returned to God by ascending in any literal sense into a heaven located somewhere above the sky."

- "I do not believe that homosexual people are abnormal, mentally sick, or morally depraved. Furthermore, I regard any sacred text that suggests otherwise to be both wrong and ill-informed."

- "I do not believe that the Bible is the 'word of God' in any literal sense."

The author of this list, posted on the Internet, is Spong, who translated a rejection of core Christianity into much fame and perhaps fortune. For many, he became the face of the contemporary Episcopal Church, and not just because of his rejection of traditional Christian belief, which endeared him to some and outraged others. Spong was also tolerated and indeed celebrated by his colleagues, and in the media, because he could be counted on for excellent quotations delivered with the certitude he found odious in his theological opponents. He was at the top of his form in an interview with journalist Barney Zwartz of *The Age* during a 2003 book tour of Australia:

- "I think there are two movements going on in the Christian faith today. One is a retreat into yesterday, into certainty and fundamentalism. It reflects the fact there is a great struggle, and they're not winning."

- "In the past God was depicted as a supernatural being who lived above the sky and periodically invaded the world to do a miracle. Then along came Copernicus and Kepler and Galileo, and suddenly the sky was empty, it was just infinite space. So the idea of God sitting above the clouds keeping record books on every individual becomes less than believable."

- "My book is an attempt to spell out a way to be Christian without checking your brains at the door of the church. You can embrace the fact that you are a citizen of the 21st century."

- "I don't believe you can manipulate God to get your will done. I refer to most prayer as adult letters to Santa Claus: 'Dear God, I've been a very good boy, please do A, B, C and D for me.' This puts God in our employ, but it didn't stop Germans killing Jews in World War II, it doesn't stop the AIDS epidemic in Africa. Mr. Bush quotes God and goes to war, and so does Osama bin Laden. There's something wrong in that equation."

Zwartz did not challenge Spong on any point, including his infantile version of God, nor did he bother to point out that Copernicus, Kepler, and Galileo were devout believers who would certainly have rejected Spong's cartoonish interpretation of their scientific insights. (Galileo remained quite devout despite his severe problems with his church.) But Zwartz did end his article with an interesting fact: "During his tenure as Bishop of Newark, confirmed communicants in the diocese virtually halved, from 44,423 in 1978, to 23,073 in 1996."

Spong's views did find critics elsewhere, often from outside his denomination. Father Gerald O'Collins, SJ, of Rome's Gregorian

University, writing in the London *Tablet* of April 30, 1994, worried that "ordinary readers who are not too familiar with modern biblical studies could easily be impressed by Spong's title of 'bishop' and his pretended scholarship." Canon Peter Jensen of the Anglican Theological College in Sydney wrote that "if this is Christianity, I would prefer to be an agnostic or atheist." John Mackey, Roman Catholic Bishop Emeritus of New Zealand, delivered perhaps the harshest blow: "The exposition of the mind of Bishop Spong reveals, I think, an attitude that a writer on Utopias, in a recent *Time* magazine, describes: 'The Utopian state of mind indicates a yearning to be released from history, to shed the burdens of free will, failure and improvisation. Basically Utopia is for authoritarians and weaklings.' Bishop Spong is among the authoritarians undoubtedly." Spong brings to my mind a canny observation attributed to a Congregationalist minister named Edmund A. Opitz: "Churchmen in every age are tempted to adopt the protective coloration of their time; like all intellectuals, churchmen are verbalists and wordsmiths; they are powerfully swayed by the printed page, by catch-words, slick phrases, slogans."

There are two crucial facts to remember when considering the larger meaning of Spong and his fellow celebrity heretics. One has to do with context, and the other, which is not often spoken about, is the fact that Spong's views are quite common not only in mainline churches but among believers often thought to be orthodox, or something close to it.

Spong is hardly the first celebrity heretic, nor is he the most profoundly heretical of that tribe. Consider very briefly the outstanding heretical achievements of Montanus and Marcion. Montanus operated in Asia Minor, Rome, Lyons, Syria, and North Africa in the mid- to late second century, and he was a man of profound visions and states of ecstasy. "I am the Father, the Word, and the Paraclete," he once declared. "I am the Lord God omnipotent." That's heresy, first class. Montanus's views go much further afield than Spong's and are indeed reminiscent of those attributed to the Rev. Sun Myung Moon. Like Moon, Montanus found a following that remained faithful even in the face of great challenges to his divine assertions. He once predicted when and where the New Jerusalem forecast in Saint John's Revelation would descend (A.D. 177, at the Phrygian village of Pepuza). This unfulfilled prediction did not kill the cult. Far from it. Constantine was battling the Montanists in 331, as was the bishop of Ephesus some two centuries after that, even though he had Montanus's bones exhumed and torched. Some traces of the cult were found as late as the eighth century.

Marcion plied his craft around Rome at roughly the same time. Marcion taught that the God of the Old Testament and the God of the New could not be one and the same. Instead, there must therefore be two Gods: the one who created the world, and the one who redeemed it. Marcion reduced the New Testament to a gutted version of Luke plus ten of Paul's letters, much as Thomas Jefferson would do some sixteen centuries later. Like Bishop Spong, Marcion rejected bodily resurrection. Yet Marcion was not interested in "widening the circle" (which one wit has interpreted as "expanding the book market"). He offered baptism only to those who were willing to abstain from worldly delights, including marriage, which he considered carnal debauchery. So strict was Marcion's aesthetic regime that it forbade wine at communion. Polycarp called him the "first born of Satan."

When placed in wider context, Spong is simply another character from what might be called America's Religious Freak Show, a group that includes Resurrection-rejecting priests, televangelists who do spiritual battle with hurricanes one moment and remove cysts from viewers' backs the next (these viewers may be several continents away), and participants in events such as the widely ridiculed "ReImagining" conference (1992), which was underwritten by the Presbyterian Church USA, the United Methodist Church, the United Church of Christ, and a few orders of nuns, among others, and featured belly-dancing seminars and deep veneration of the earth goddess Sophia, to whom a somewhat erotic prayer was offered: "Our maker Sophia, we are women in your image. . . . With the hot blood of our wombs we give form to new life. . . . With nectar between our thighs we invite a lover, we birth a child; with our warm body fluids we remind the world of its pleasures and sensations. . . . We celebrate the sweat that pours from us during our labors. We celebrate the fingertips vibrating upon the skin of a lover."

Spong does differ from earlier heretics, however, in that they often paid a price for their unconventional ideas, including expulsion and sometimes much worse. By contrast, these views have paid Spong a high dividend. More important, however, is the fact that Bishop Spong's views, while harshly criticized in some quarters as being far beyond the pale, are present not only throughout the mainline but throughout Protestantism, even in churches that are assumed to maintain traditional theological rigor. By some counts there are more people in the pews with views similar to Spong's than with views that adhere to the traditional Creed.

Barna Research, a California polling and marketing company that focuses on religious belief in the United States, has observed that about half of Protestant pastors agree with Spong regarding at least some traditional teachings and beliefs. Barna asked pastors a selection of questions: Did they believe in absolute moral truth as revealed in the Bible? Did they believe that Jesus was without sin? Did they believe Satan literally exists? Did they believe God is omnipotent and omniscient? Did they believe that Christians must evangelize? All told, only 28 percent of pastors from mainline Protestant churches answered all the questions in the affirmative. Only 15 percent of female pastors said yes in every case. Meanwhile, out in the pews, only 7 percent of Americans said yes to all these questions, and among born-again Christians the number was only 9 percent.

So far as the clergy goes, these departures from orthodox belief are not the result of a lack of seminary education. To the contrary. Barna also found that pastors who had attended a seminary were less likely to have a biblical worldview (45 percent) than those who skipped seminary altogether (59 percent). As we shall see in chapter 6, one study found that the longer seminarians stayed in liberalized Baptist seminaries, the more likely they were to abandon traditional beliefs.

Barna also found that born-again Christians, who are often portrayed as assertive fundamentalists and proselytizers, are quite different from what their stereotype suggests. Twenty-eight percent of born-agains, for example, agreed that "while he lived on earth, Jesus committed sins, like other people." That is far from a fundamentalist belief. Even further afield, 35 percent did not believe Jesus experienced a physical resurrection, putting them in company not only with Bishop Spong but with 39 percent of the general population. (Eighty-five percent of Americans said they believe that Jesus is "spiritually alive," whatever that might mean.) Sixty-one percent of adult Americans believed the Holy Spirit is merely a symbol of God's presence or power and not a living entity; a majority of born-again Christians (52 percent) felt the same way. Nor did the Devil find much support among this group of believers. Nearly 60 percent of American adults said Satan does not exist as a being at all but is merely a symbol of evil; 45 percent of born-again Christians agreed. Among Protestants who attended non-mainline churches, only half believed in Satan. Disbelief in a personified and marauding Evil may reflect American optimism, as may the finding that four of five Americans believe in angels. And while Scripture suggests—strongly suggests, by some readings—that few will enter the Kingdom of Heaven, only one-half of 1 percent of Americans said there's the slightest chance they'll end up in hell.

It is also clear, from Barna's research, that these allegedly hardcore and threatening Christians, who are portrayed as the storm troopers of the religious right, have very little interest in bringing nonbelievers into the fold. Over one-quarter—26 percent—thought that it doesn't matter what faith a person has because religions teach pretty much the same thing, while 50 percent believed that a life of "good works" will get one into heaven. A host of other departures from the stereotype have also been discovered by Barna. Born-again Christians, who are rumored to marry their childhood sweethearts (whom they likely met at church) and never depart from them, in fact experienced divorce at higher rates than non-Christians. Nor are they uniformly Republican. According to 2001 figures, 38 percent of Democrats, 57 percent of Republicans, and 35 percent of independents consider themselves born-again Christians. Political analyst and writer Steve Waldman has reminded us that "at least 10 million white evangelical Christians voted for Gore." They also are not lightly educated or poor, as some of their detractors would have us believe:

- Of the 12 million evangelical adults in the United States, 29 percent have a college degree, a figure that is higher than the national average.

- The share of adult born-again Christians from households making $60,000 or more annually rose from 13 percent in

1991 to 25 percent in 2000. The percentage of Asians who are born-again grew from 5 to 27 percent over the past decade—a 440 percent increase.

Some Americans may find much to celebrate in these numbers, including those who, along with Rector Gray, fear the onslaught of an army of marauding born-agains and evangelicals led by a theocratic billionaire. These numbers indicate not only a lack of crusading spirit but a lack of a unifying set of beliefs that would inspire such a spirit. Interestingly enough, Barna also found that theological inconsistency and incoherence are not restricted to believers. About half the atheists and agnostics polled believed that human beings have souls and that there is life after death. "One out of every eight atheists and agnostics even believe that accepting Jesus Christ as savior probably makes life after death possible," George Barna of Barna Research noted, adding that he considered this to be "further evidence that many Americans adopt simplistic views of life and the afterlife based upon ideas drawn from disparate sources, such as movies, music and novels, without carefully considering those beliefs."

Other pollsters and analysts have noted the incoherence and shallowness of religious belief in America. Christian writer Eddie Gibbs published a book entitled *In Name Only* (1994) in which he pointed out that "the knowledge base of traditional Christian belief is alarmingly vague and narrow, and for 90 percent of churchgoers belief is not translated into distinctive Christian values and lifestyle. Many professing Christians live lives which are indistinguishable from those persons who are not active churchgoers or who profess no Christian commitment. This state of affairs gives some substance to the cynical remark that 'religion in North America is 3,000 miles wide and three inches deep.'" That observation finds backing in another Barna finding: 60 percent of Americans believe the Bible "is totally accurate in all its teachings." This indicates that most Americans aren't too sure what the Bible teaches about the nature of evil, absolute truth, and the specifics of the Resurrection.

But most Americans are quite sure they are fully informed about the nature of God. All told, 70 percent of Americans believe God is an "all-powerful, all knowing, perfect creator that rules the world today." This is not the God of the celebrity heretics. This is the ancient God who lives in the Old and New Testaments and who is worshiped in traditionalist churches, whether Southern Baptist, Roman Catholic, or Orthodox, along with many nondenominational churches and Pentecostal congregations. This is the God that serious believers, and many nonbelievers as well, want their children to worship or at least learn about, even if, in the latter case, they find the claims made on His behalf to be hard to grasp, far-fetched, or perhaps even untenable. They recognize that belief in such a God is somehow central to a deeper happiness, that belief in such a God supplies their children with a survival tool they cannot get elsewhere. This is the God that sustains. This God has drawing power and continues to sap the mainline of serious believers and attract those seeking a deity they can respect. Of course, by orthodox standards, this is God, period.

This is most definitely not the God found in the more advanced regions of progressive religion, including the Unitarian-Universalist Church, where I wanted to stop on my way to my first visit with refugees from the mainline.

For many progressives, belief in an all-powerful God is not possible, and not desirable. Better to find a slighter deity such as the one conjured up by "process theologians." As author Wendy Murray Zorba explained in *Christianity Today*, these innovators have reduced God to about one-third of His former self. This God, according to a former enthusiast named Royce Gordon Gruenler, is quite limited. He "does not know the future. He has ideals for the future, and he tries to lure us to actualize those ideals, but he does not control each individual or occasion on the atomic scale." Indeed, this deity is often adrift and in need of an anchor, however unsteady. "God needs us because without us he's not concrete. He sets the ideals, but then we create the content and God expands his actuality through us. We add to him." Because God is not fully realized, He is "in process."

This 30 percent God is a Wee Deity—WD-30, we might call Him—and attractive in the sense that no one need fear such a God, or heed Him either. The problem, however, is that such a God is not much of a God at all. His hands are tied by the deficiency of His very nature. "If God is limited to our time," Gruenler eventually concluded, "that means he's constrained to move at 186,000 miles per second—the speed of light. That's a very slow time for God to be synthesizing everything in the universe instantaneously, as process theology posits. The moment you say that, you enter irrationality." Besides that, Gruenler added, "because we are free agents—agents that act on our own—God cannot only *not have* the future as actual, he cannot have the present as actual either. The present is where you are doing your actualizing by your own free agency. So God only truly has your past. He has only fossils to work with." Bottom line: "What percentage of power, then, does God have in this scheme? Does he have 20 percent and the advancing world has the other 80 percent? Is it 30/70? And if that's the case, why is he worth worshiping?" Gruenler, a clergyman, was forced by these conclusions to return to Christian orthodoxy. "I was in the church preaching lousy, liberal sermons, and the church was dying."

The lesser the God, the smaller the congregation. The

Unitarian-Universalist Church is proof of that. To be sure, for some Unitarians a 30 percent God is at least 25 percent or so too much. That turned out to be the case during one Sunday morning visit.

The Unitarians play a cherished role for many commentators, especially those of a conservative nature. A Baptist leader we shall visit in chapter 6 calls them "secularists with steeples." They are famous for worshiping one God, at most. They also represent what is probably the purest form of progressive Christianity to be found in America. The Unitarians may now be where the mainliners end up.

Corporately known as the Unitarian-Universalist Association (UUA), this church refuses to officially acknowledge the existence of a heavenly Father, Mother, or Significant Other. This has created dissidents, though not many. I came across two a few years ago while doing research for a newspaper article. David Burton and Dean Fisher had attracted an editor's eye not only because both were theistic Unitarians but also because they were trying to bring God back into the Unitarian fold. A tough assignment, as I was to find. Burton calculated that "at least half of Unitarians are now atheists," and he complained that while political activists, witches, pagans, and atheists find a warm home in UUA churches, traditionally theistic Unitarians, especially Christians, often confront open hostility. "And let's face it," he added, "an atheistic church really is an oxymoron. We think the church should explore the nature of the divine, but it is much more interested in exploring the nature of politics."

Politics, or at least liberal politics, is the Unitarian passion, but the chief object of worship is the human being. According to the UUA's Web site, "In the end, religious authority lies not in a book, person, or institution, but in ourselves." Pop-up ads bear similar messages: "Instead of me fitting a religion, I found a religion to fit me," and, "You don't have to see God as straight, white, and a man." While such pitches to individualism seem custom-ordered

for our day, there are only 155,000 Unitarians in the United
States—216,000 if you count children. By comparison, there are
200,000 adult converts to Catholicism in America in any given
year.

The Unitarian tradition has not always been thus. It includes
deeply devout Christians, including P. T. Barnum, whose best-known
contributions to American culture included the promotion of Tom
Thumb and the "Fejee Mermaid"—a creature advertised as a bare-
breasted beauty of the deep that turned out, on further inspection,
to be a monkey's head sewn to the body of a fish.

Yet Barnum was a deeply religious Christian whose faith
guided his public life. "I have been indebted to Christianity for the
most serene happiness of my life," Barnum wrote in his autobiography, "and I would not part with its consolations for all things else
in the world." He was, according to biographer A. H. Saxon, the
chief supporter of the First Universalist Society in Bridgeport,
Connecticut, for over forty years. Universalism was then considered a liberal form of Christianity, primarily because it rejected the
belief that only a small elect will find salvation. Its profession of
faith, however, was fundamentalist compared with what has followed. It recognized "one God, whose nature is Love, revealed in
one Lord Jesus Christ, by one Holy Spirit of Grace, who will finally restore the whole family of mankind to holiness and happiness." It was an animating faith as well, one that inspired Barnum
to embrace unpopular causes. He strongly opposed capital punish-
ment and while a member of the Connecticut legislature was a
strong advocate for the enfranchisement of African Americans.

P. T. Barnum had not yet entered show business when Richmond's first Universalist church was formed in 1830. It faced immediate "resentment toward liberal identification," according to
its publicity materials and so changed its name to the First Independent Christian Church. This brought some measure of peace

until 1862, when the church's minister was arrested as a "Union sympathizer" and "probable spy." The church shut down, and the Universalists were without a formal home until 1893, when the First Unitarian Church of Richmond was founded. It would face, however, "a struggle for survival and a continual debt," which eventually resulted in the church's nearly collapsing once again. The early twentieth century also brought "hard times both for the country and liberal religion." Somehow, though apparently not by the Grace of God (God is not mentioned in this history or in other promotional literature the church makes available), First Unitarian persevered and now boasts some 450 members. "The church has an important stable and religious role in the life of Richmond area religious liberals," it says. "Still a center of challenging and rational thought, still featuring the best art show in Richmond, and still engaged in community improvement projects and forums, the church has slowly become more diverse in thought and belief and program and has opened to new religious styles and made vital connection with other religious groups in England, Europe and Japan."

This sense of struggle in the face of religious chauvinism, sustained only by the knowledge of superior intelligence and taste, was very much present the mornings I visited First Unitarian.

One service began with a short piece by Debussy, played with minimal errors on a piano. A lone candle glowed atop a lectern; there were about fifty adults present, dressed casually. The service was led by a guest speaker who convened a short period of meditation. That segment ended when she sounded a small bell. The sounding involuntarily elicited in this visitor an unspoken declarative sentence: "Dinner is served!" Our leader—tall, brunette, and somewhere in her thirties—looked about the dimly lit room and announced that we are all "born in mystery and die in mystery," yet in the intervening years we can engage in communal life that al-

lows us to "activate our creative possibilities." Unitarianism, she
continued enthusiastically, is the perfect sort of faith for this world,
for it is "so independent and unique."

These opening words were followed by a hymn titled "As
Tranquil Streams," which included this verse:

> *Free from the bonds that bind the mind*
> *To narrow thought and lifeless creed*
> *Free from a social code that fails*
> *To serve the cause of human need*

Then came the time for the principal message. The topic was
posed in the form of a question: "Do we have what it takes to be a
sustaining faith?" The leader began by observing that many people
do not believe Unitarianism qualifies as a sustaining faith. This
belief is also reflected, she added, in the fact that the church has a
difficult time keeping young people in the fold. Many of them
complain that it "cannot sustain them in hard times."

Yet her own experience had taught a different lesson. She had
been a chaplain in a northern hospital and had faced many traumatic circumstances, including the need to counsel dying patients.
And she had done a good job, she believed, even though some patients preferred the services of the more mainstream Christian
chaplains. These stricken people "longed for greater assurance of
an afterlife," but she could not help them, for she did not believe in
an afterlife—or, for that matter, in God, 30 percent or otherwise.
The other chaplains, she continued, "had an answer for everything. All I had were questions."

I couldn't help but imagine a stricken patient, perhaps an old
woman devastated by a ferocious malignancy, who had sought
some measure of eternal consolation from this chaplain. One wonders what the harm could be in giving that assurance to a suffering

person, no matter what your personal belief. Not doing so seemed inhumane.

The audience chuckled at the mention of an afterlife and God and listened quietly—perhaps reverently—when she added that she had been able to "reach out" to many troubled people she met in the hospital, including two parents who had been brought in with a grievously injured child. The child, she said, was thought to have been shaken by the parents and was close to death. While other staff members bombarded the parents with glares of "hatred," she alone had "reached out" to them, for she alone had been able to recognize "the dignity and potential for good in all." And that, she concluded, is a sustaining philosophy.

On her behalf, however, she was simply remaining faithful to her creed, as laid out in the Unitarian-Universalist principles:

WE BELIEVE
- that each and every person is important
- that all people should be treated fairly and kindly
- that we should accept one another and keep on learning
- that each person must be free to search for what is true and right in life
- that all persons should have a vote about the things that concern them
- in working for a peaceful, fair and free world
- in caring for our planet Earth, the home we share with all living things

There is no hope for the dying in this creed. And as our speaker pointed out, it offers little hope for struggling children either. The latter admission seemed more startling on further reflection, especially in contrast to the view of orthodox believers, one of whose primary concerns is to imbue their children with a faith that will sustain them through difficulty. Because my interest in religion includes its biological origins and nature—that is, its central role in helping humans not only personally survive but also, through the creation and nurture of children, project their genetic component into the future—this admission took on a chilling nature. This may be a faith that glories in the individual, an attitude that most Americans can appreciate. At the same time, it also seems to be a faith that has embraced extinction, or something quite close to it. Or, as other commentators have noted, the more thoroughly a church embraces this world, the smaller its congregation, and perhaps its life span as well.

I departed as the collection basket was started around the room. In the foyer a young man sat at a table reading a book. The table was a distribution point for various pamphlets and circulars dedicated to "peace and justice issues." I asked him what he was reading, wondering whether it might possibly be a religious or philosophical work. He smiled and held up the cover: *Citizen Cohn* by Nicholas Von Hoffman.

It was now time to move into traditionalist territory.

If we think of the churches in America's religious spectrum as a collection of familiar structures, the Unitarians might best be represented by a pup tent. If we now imagine the Superdome, we have fixed our eyes on the largest branch of Christianity, the Roman Catholic Church. Some have likened the Catholic Church to a great magnet that exerts a slow but ultimately irresistible tug on serious Christians, including those in flight from mainline Protestant denominations. I know a few former Episcopalians who have taken the path to Rome. They believe they have found the castle keep of Christianity.

These are indeed serious believers who desire a faith worthy of their commitment. They have gone from a micro church to a massive church. But as I was to find, they do not see themselves as part of an organization whose sheer size ensures cultural domination, respect, or security. To the contrary. Several of them believe they have taken the path of greatest resistance, one that may eventually place them and their families in mortal danger. Somewhere in the future may lurk another Nero, or worse. Some believe that future is not far off.

But they do have the assurance that in the fullness of time all will be well. Such is the promise given them by their church, which like other traditionalist churches holds fast to the ancient texts, including the magisterial Nicene Creed. I reread a version on the way to my first interview with a mainline refugee. I had forgotten what a beautiful piece of work it is:

> *I believe in one God the Father Almighty, Maker of heaven and earth, and of all things visible and invisible. And in one Lord Jesus Christ, the only begotten Son of God, begotten of His Father before all worlds; God of God, Light of Light; Very God of Very God; Begotten, not made: Being of one substance with the Father, by whom all things were made; Who for us men, and for our salvation, came down from heaven; And was incarnate by the Holy Ghost of the Virgin Mary, and was made man; And was crucified also for us under Pontius Pilate. He suffered and was buried; And the third day He rose again according to the Scriptures; and ascended into heaven; And sitteth on the right hand of the Father. And he shall come again with glory to judge both the quick and the dead; Whose kingdom shall have no end. And I believe in the Holy Ghost; the Lord and Giver of Life; Who proceedeth from the Father and the Son; Who with the Fa-*

ther and the Son together is worshiped and glorified; Who spoke by the prophets. And I believe in one Holy Catholic and Apostolic Church. I acknowledge one Baptism for the remission of sins. And I look for the Resurrection of the dead; And the Life of the world to come. Amen.

Part Two

The Abiding Hope

Four

The Catholic Church

Some Roads Lead to Rome

There are many mansions in the Christian household, and none is grander than the Catholic Church. This is the Big House, with more members worldwide than any other branch of the faith and a history that is central to the history of the West. Denounced by its many critics as a monolith, it is in fact one of the most diverse of all human institutions. It counts among its members the greatest scientific, artistic, and humanitarian minds the world has known, as well as zealots eager to censor and commit torture unto death. Some of its thinkers have embraced Marxism, and others are among the most compelling apostles of market capitalism. It is also the religious destination for many refugees from the mainline train wreck. When heretics make headlines, they are also making Catholics, and very good Catholics at that. Some take a long while to reach Rome, but once there they have joined not only the ancients but the rapidly expanding Catholic population of the Southern Hemisphere. Before many more decades pass, those who fear Catholic power may find themselves pining for the days when all they had to worry about was a tunnel connecting the Vatican to the White House.

Catholicism, to be sure, remains a warm home for some of the world's most vigorous leftists. Pax Christi, which calls itself "the Catholic Peace Voice," continues making the type of moral equivalence arguments popular during the cold war: "More people die each year crossing the U.S.-Mexico border than died during 28 years trying to cross the Berlin Wall," stated a bulletin on the organization's Web site. In the run-up to the 2004 elections, PC (as some call it) sold shirts advertising its "efforts to monitor the upcoming Florida elections. On the front are the words 'Every Vote, Every Voter Counts in 2004,' and on the back are the words, 'Fair U.S. Elections: Brought to you by International Election Monitors.' Join with us in this campaign by wearing these shirts to show your support for our international election monitors!"

But the dynamism is on the right, in two senses. In the Southern Hemisphere, Catholicism is growing rapidly, as we shall see later in this chapter, as is evangelical Christianity. Southern Hemisphere Catholics, for the most part, are what one prominent Catholic leader calls "with the program." They regularly attend Mass and Confession and make a serious effort to conform their lives to church teachings. In a finding that will curdle liberal blood, scholar Philip Jenkins suggests that these deeply conservative Catholics promise to play a decisive role in church politics. The other interesting dynamic is the influx of high-profile American conservatives into the Catholic church, including journalist Robert Novak, senator Sam Brownback, economist Larry Kudlow, columnist Laura Ingraham, jurist (and now law professor) Robert Bork, publisher Al Regnery, and cultural commentator Andrew Ferguson. Thus is formed a conservative religious coalition between black and brown Southern Hemisphere Catholics and white American conservatives—somewhat reminiscent of the growing alliance between mostly white American conservative Episcopalians and black African bishops, though on a grander scale.

What draws these conservatives to Catholicism? What do they

find in Rome that they could not find elsewhere? I wanted to ask that question of Father John McCloskey, who has played a central role in many of these high-profile conversions, along with many hundreds of others. Why does his church appeal to men like Robert Novak and Robert Bork, both of whom were well-known skeptics and, in the latter case especially, powerful intellectuals? How can a church whose teachings precede by many centuries the age of reason and modern science command their allegiance?

First, however, I wanted to talk with refugees from the mainline. I personally knew two who had come to Rome by way of the Episcopal and Anglican Churches: conservative publisher Al Regnery and journalist Andrew Ferguson. The latter's story is touched on in the introduction: Ferguson is the poor soul who found himself to be a lonely theist in an Episcopal seminary.

I have known Andy Ferguson over twenty years. We met when he was working at *The American Spectator,* where he had a sometimes stormy experience. Andy would go on to greater things, including writing speeches for President George Herbert Walker Bush, essays for *Time* magazine, columns for Bloomberg News, and articles for Rupert Murdoch's *Weekly Standard.* I had known him to be a churchgoing Anglican who studied at the Episcopal seminary in Berkeley while attending the University of California at Berkeley. Prior to that, he had played in a Los Angeles rock-and-roll band. He likes Scotch and martinis, though not necessarily in that order. He is a student of the life of Abraham Lincoln. And, he told me a short time back, he had joined the Catholic Church.

I asked him why he had done so.

The story began in that seminary. It is no doubt widely assumed that people go to seminary to deepen their knowledge of God and the creeds and practices of the denomination they hope to serve. An outsider would reasonably expect seminarians to have a deeper religious aptitude or talent, as it were, just as the student at a conservatory is assumed to be in possession of a more powerful musical aptitude than someone who simply strums a guitar for his or her own occasional pleasure. If the seminarian plans to lead a congregation, he or she will have taken up the task of keeping the flame of faith burning and on any given day must be prepared to make the case for God to a congregant whose confrontation with tragedy has triggered a crisis of faith. They must give assurance to the dying (unless perhaps they happen to be Unitarians) and comfort the afflicted with the promise that all will be well.

Or so many of us would assume. But the fact is, these days attending a Christian seminary can be hazardous to one's faith. Andy Ferguson discovered this firsthand.

One day at San Francisco's Church Divinity School of the Pacific, Andy engaged in a spirited exchange with a favorite professor. This was not the first such engagement. "We would have furious arguments about basic tenets of the traditional faith," he began in his northern Virginia living room. "These were the sorts of things mentioned, you know, in the Nicene Creed." The operating assumption throughout the seminary, Andy continued, was that "all religions are essentially the same" and that "it doesn't matter if Jesus rose from the dead." Jesus didn't walk on water, cast out demons, or spring from the womb of a teenage virgin. Instead, "Jesus was a good man who merely showed us that we have to learn to triumph over adversity." The sorts of beliefs, we can reasonably say, that are easily picked up without the help of a seminary education.

After this particular exchange, Andy went to the lunchroom and sat down for a bowl of soup. "A guy from class came over and asked if he could join me. I said sure, so he sat down and said, 'We've been talking about you. We know you're having a rough time, and we've finally figured out what your problem is.'"

What would that be? Andy asked.

"You're the only one here who believes in God."

"And you know what?" Andy said as he sat forward in his easy chair. "He was right. They believed in things like the redemptive power of the universe, but I was the last one there who wanted to defend the biblical God—the God who makes claims on us, who said we should do some things and not do others, and who put each of us here for a purpose."

Andy had once entertained the idea of becoming a priest, but by now that idea had lost its appeal. And so Andy focused on writing, eventually making his way to Washington as conservatives laid siege to the city during the first administration of Ronald Reagan, a Presbyterian who rarely made it to church but did cut taxes, build up the military, and invoke God more than enough to convince jittery liberals that the man with his finger on the nuclear trigger very much believed in Armageddon and feared it not.

Andy would visit a church from time to time, and one day he found himself in a "classic" Episcopal church on O Street in downtown Washington. This was a "providential day," he recalled, though it didn't seem to start that way. "They were using the new prayer book, which combines flat, pedestrian language with new age gibberish," Andy said (as a cultural commentator, he wields a sharp pen and tongue). Then came time for the priest to deliver the day's message. "It was a sermon in support of the Sandinistas. I swear." Andy rose from the pew and was soon walking down O Street. Then Providence showed its hand. "I walked past this little church, and the signboard outside said, WE USE THE OLD PRAYER BOOK. This was a little schismatic church that had broken away from the Episcopal Church in the 1970s." Not only did the church use the old prayer book. It had a fairly young and very dynamic rector: the Rev. John Cahoon. He was, Andy believed, the agent of

Providence. At the very least, he was a priest who believed not only in God but also in the traditional Christian view of God.

The Rev. Cahoon had one other thing going for him, at least from Andy's perspective. He did not share Andy's political conservatism. "He was very left-wing—a Jesse Jackson guy. But that was important because it taught me that religion is detached from Republican Party politics. Religion is much, much deeper." Cahoon did share Andy's love of good writing and the traditional liturgy, which, he said, "puts you into a spiritual rhythm. It takes you through the seasons of the year in their relation to the life of Christ. I like the idea of a liturgy that has formed over the centuries. I believe it is more trustworthy than some guy standing up there extemporizing."

Cahoon's homilies, however insightful, elevated, and short they might be ("none over four minutes"), were often sharply focused on contemporary events, including what Cahoon called the "scandal" under way in the modern Episcopal Church. Cahoon had been in San Francisco the day Bishop James Pike made heresy safe for Episcopal priests, an event mentioned in chapter 2. This was, Cahoon believed, a defining moment. Among other things, it signaled the end of the denomination as a dependable transmitter of Christian truth. That role, from his perspective, was the reason for the church's existence.

Cahoon was a forceful defender of the traditional faith. In a series of Eastertide sermons in 1999, he reminded his congregation that Easter does not commemorate a gauzy "spiritual resurrection" or serve as Christianity's version of an ancient fertility pageant. "The resurrection of Jesus is not a symbol of the rebirth of nature in spring. The rebirth of nature in spring is a symbol of the resurrection of Jesus." He quoted the old hymn "Welcome, Happy Morning":

Bloom in every meadow, leaves on every bough
Speak his sorrow ended, hail his triumph now.

"We shall come up out of our own graves when he comes back," Cahoon promised, with a certitude that would make the stones guffaw back at the Church Divinity School of the Pacific. He understood, however, that some believers in Christian pews were hearing a different story, and as an antidote he advised a close study of Mark's Gospel. "If we are rooted in his teaching we will not be, to quote the collect, 'Like children carried away with every blast of vain doctrine' [or] susceptible to any attractive new idea and any sort of deceptive trickery someone might use to try to get us off the right path. Flightiness in beliefs and actions and susceptibility to anything new are the prevailing sins of our period of history—especially in the church."

This was all a lead-up to Cahoon's Easter morning pounding of the progressives who had forced traditionalists to form schismatic churches. "When a priest is consecrated bishop," Cahoon began, "he is told, quite bluntly, 'Be to the flock of Christ a shepherd, not a wolf: feed them, devour them not.' I used to have a friend who was fond of saying, 'When the Devil wants to wreck the church, he gets the clergy to do it for him.' Our own church has had to come into existence because of a vulpine plague of bad shepherds. Bishops have a number of responsibilities. One of them is to confirm people, as I am here to do this evening, but my main responsibility is to tell you that Jesus Christ is risen from the dead—and that if you are in him, you will rise from the dead too. A church which tolerates bishops who deny the resurrection has no claim to be a real church at all."

Cahoon's effect on Andy's faith was profound. "I was totally revitalized," Andy said. He had been brought back to life, in a spiritual sense. But John Cahoon's life took an unforeseen turn. He had developed brain cancer, which was discovered late. He died in August 2001, at age fifty-two, a refugee from his beloved Episcopal Church.

After Cahoon's death came a reevaluation. What, Andy asked himself, is truly important in matters spiritual? The prayer book is "a masterpiece of prose," and the Anglican service "is the most beautiful of all Christian services," Andy concluded, but in fact they cannot be considered "essential religion." John Cahoon was a great man and a great priest, but the Christian religion is not about individual star-power. It is about Truth, and his allegiance, Andy thought, should go to the church that is the most dependable and well-grounded protector of that Truth. The breakaway Traditional Anglican Communion is a good church, but also something of a refugee center. Once again, Andy found himself in a spiritual wilderness.

Then, he said, the hand of Providence once again fell upon him. Andy and his wife Denise had enrolled their son and daughter in a local Catholic school, a choice made by many non-Catholics with little faith in the public school system. "I put him to bed the first night of school, and as I was walking out the door he said, 'Dad, did you know Mary is the mother of God?' A chill went up and down my spine. I said to myself, 'My God, they go to work on them fast.'" As it happened, the "Catholic tug" would become quite strong from that night forward. The transition from Anglo-Catholicism to Catholicism did not require a major liturgical leap, though Andy is still somewhat bothered by "the papacy and Mary worship." But those were small matters, he said. In the greater scheme of things, Catholicism not only offers a sound liturgy but stands firm where other faiths no longer do. The Catholic Church "deserves allegiance because it is a bulwark against a lot of the rotten things like euthanasia, abortion, and the devaluation of life," Andy said. The full embrace of this aspect of the faith requires an end to "unnatural" birth control methods and also marks one as an enemy of unfettered personal autonomy. As such, a devoted Catholic is something of an outlaw in his own age, at least in this country.

Andy agreed. "Catholicism makes many demands," he replied, "and the most profound demand is for intellectual submission. The church believes there is such a thing as right and wrong, that there is such a thing as sin, and there is such a thing as judgment. You can never be 100 percent certain on your own account. That is why you must submit to the church. That is where certitude lies, in an unbroken line two thousand years old." Submission, he agreed, is "counter to the American way." But it is in keeping with Christianity's central lesson, he added. "If you take Jesus seriously, you will be constantly reminded that the humbled are exalted, and the exalted are brought low. Christianity is a constant reminder to humans that 'you are not God.' It is the most subversive power ever unleashed in the universe."

As our time drew short, I asked his views on his old church, mentioning my conversation with Hugo Blankingship Jr. "Blankingship's generation was the tolerant generation," Andy replied. "Theirs was the generation that allowed the people who are now in power to come into power. But will the group now in power be so tolerant of Blankingship and anyone else who opposes their views? It looks like they won't."

He agreed with Blankingship that a lack of authority has played a crucial part in the Episcopal Church's decline. "Bishop Pike proclaimed himself a heretic and challenged the Episcopal Church to do something about it. The church did nothing. John Cahoon was right. If a church can't enforce its standards even to the point of getting rid of someone like Bishop Pike, then it is doomed." In fact, Andy added, the entire mainline is doomed, at least as a home for serious believers. "Mainline Protestantism will reach a certain point where it will appeal only to Wiccans, vegetarians, sandal-wearers, and people who play the recorder. No one will feel at home there if they believe in God. But it won't disappear. It has too much money to totally go away." He waited a second, then said, "It's good to see these puffed-up Episcopalians humbled. They became creatures of the world. This is what they deserve."

I mentioned that the Catholic Church was currently mortgaging properties in order to pay off victims who had been sexually abused by priests. How could such a thing happen in the Mother Church? Andy seemed ready for the question. He chalked the troubles up to a "huge influx of homosexuals into the seminaries after Vatican II" and credited John Paul II with sending emissaries in the late 1980s to extirpate the cabal and restore order. And there is, he emphasized, a great deal of order in his church that will not be changing anytime soon. The Fergusons attend St. Agnes in northern Virginia. There are no altar girls, and, he added, there will never be women priests. "Back during the push for women priests in the Episcopal Church, there were warnings that this would lead to the leveling of all sexual differences, and that in the end it would open the pulpit to homosexuals. Everyone of course said that was hysterical, but we now know that it was true."

There is no doubting the completeness of Andy's conversion or his disdain for the church he left behind, which he reiterated in an e-mail the day after our meeting. "You know, after you left, I had one other thought that I wish I'd gotten across to you, which is that I think this conservative Episcopalian obsession with homosexuality—using it as an excuse to leave the church—is just bizarre. These right-wingers have put up with every kind of heresy and modish innovation in their communion for thirty years, including the de facto acceptance of adultery and the explicit acceptance of abortion and euthanasia, and suddenly someone gets nice to [gays] and they decide it's an insult to the faith? I don't like the word 'homophobe,' but I do think these guys fit the term."

In an earlier day, Andy Ferguson might well have become an Episcopal priest, one deeply committed to that church's traditions and an energetic contributor to its Christian mission in the world. One easily imagines he would have turned out at least a few highly literate and engaging volumes defending and promoting that mission, volumes that would have inspired other bright and talented men and women to join the priestly ranks. It is on such people that strong churches are built.

There is no way of knowing how many people like Andy Ferguson have been driven away from the Episcopal Church by its theological and social innovations. We do know that people of his intelligence and talent are rare and that the loss of even one can have far-reaching effects in a denomination, especially a small one. As I went to my next interview I thought of the words of Dr. Baillie, the old Episcopal priest mentioned in chapter 3, who noted the high price paid for "proud illusions." Andy, and people like him, are the absent priests for those vacant pews.

Al Regnery, another former Episcopalian, has also answered the Roman tug. I wondered if his reasons were the same as Andy's, or if there was a different or additional attraction. That seemed likely. Andy is a writer, and Al is a longtime publisher. He is also a quiet man who has nonetheless made an important contribution to America's political life.

Regnery Books was perhaps the most subversive publishing company of the second half of the twentieth century, at least in the area of public policy and cultural affairs. While mainstream publishers insisted that they were not ideologically motivated, their inattention to the interests of conservative book buyers created a market that Regnery exploited with great success. Though small and something of an outlaw organization, the company regularly published bestsellers. Al Regnery became president of Regnery Gateway in 1986, and that company became Regnery Publishing in 1993 (the company's original name was the Henry Regnery Company). Under his auspices, twenty-two books became *New York Times* bestsellers.

Regnery also republished some of the classics of the cold war era, including Whittaker Chambers's *Witness*, which enjoyed a resurgence of popularity in the 1980s, in no small part owing to the fact that one of its greatest admirers was Ronald Reagan, who was known to recite long passages from *Witness* and sometimes included those passages in his speeches. "Letter to My Children," which served as *Witness*'s prologue, achieved creedal reverence among conservatives, especially those who considered the cold war to be, at heart, a war between atheism and Christianity. Chambers, whose stormy life on both sides of the political and sexual divides made him an especially interesting and important witness, closed his letter with a paragraph of enduring beauty:

> *My children, when you were little, we used sometimes to go for walks in our pine woods. In the open fields, you would run along by yourselves. But you used instinctively to give me your hands as we entered those woods, where it was darker, lonelier, and in the stillness our voices sounded loud and frightening. In this book I am again giving you my hands. I am leading you, not through cool pine woods, but up and up a narrow defile between bare and steep rocks from which in shadow things uncoil and slither away. It will be dark. But, in the end, if I have led you aright, you will make out three crosses, from two of which hang thieves. I will*

have brought you to Golgotha—the place of skulls. This is the meaning of the journey. Before you understand, I may not be there, my hands may have slipped from yours. It will not matter. For when you understand what you see, you will no longer be children. You will know that life is pain, that each of us hangs always upon the cross of himself. And when you know that this is true of every man woman and child on earth, you will be wise.

In 2003 Al Regnery left his job in an attempt to rescue the struggling *American Spectator*. We met at the *Spectator*'s new offices in Rosslyn, Virginia, just across the Potomac River from Washington. Al wore a dark suit and was hard at work when I arrived.

I asked about his religious background. His mother came from a family of Philadelphia Quakers. His father was not particularly interested in church. But the family was deeply involved in the long struggle with Soviet communism and in the conservative movement in general. These were their friends, and their customers. He got around to joining the Episcopal Church in the early 1980s, attending for a time the Falls Church in northern Virginia, known for its conservative leanings and membership. But Regnery saw the denomination crumbling around him. Homosexuality was not only tolerated, as it should be, but celebrated. If traditions derived from Scripture conflicted with contemporary liberalism, it was no contest. "In the final analysis," Regnery said, "the Episcopal Church has lots of good people in it, but it just doesn't stand for anything."

The Catholic Church was different, he was coming to discover. A priest named Father John McCloskey, who had very conservative leanings of his own, had invited Regnery along on some retreats. He also recommended works by Catholic scholars and writers from a reading list he had compiled, and he made himself available to answer questions about the faith. Regnery, as it turns out, was in very capable hands. John McCloskey has brought hundreds of people into the church by the most modest count, including several who would make the A-list for any conservative publisher: Robert Bork, Robert Novak, Larry Kudlow, Senator Sam Brownback, and Laura Ingraham.

Andy Ferguson had been strongly attracted by the church's historic and consistent liturgy, which Regnery made very little mention of. He was deeply impressed, however, by an encounter he witnessed between church officials and a group of hospital administrators. "The hospital people were saying the church needed to change its position against allowing abortions in Catholic hospitals," Regnery explained. "The church said that was not going to happen. Period. The administrators were shocked. They said this position was costing the hospitals tens of millions of dollars. After the meeting I got in a cab with a few people from the hospital group. They didn't know who I was and started talking about what had just happened. They just couldn't believe the church would take a stand that would cost them so much money." Turning down profit because of principle made a deep impression on this businessman.

Regnery was also impressed by the size of the institution. "There's probably a Mass being said somewhere in the world every second of every day," he said. He also found Catholics to be more forgiving of personal foibles than some of his acquaintances in the other branches of the faith. "I had a source in the White House who told me that the last-minute revelation during the 2000 elections of George W. Bush's DUI cost him a lot of votes among evangelicals," said Regnery. "That's just not a Catholic attitude."

Commitment to principle, institutional vastness, and a forgiving attitude helped persuade Regnery to become a Catholic; he was accepted into the church in August 2002. Living up to his taciturn reputation, he indicated that this was the entirety of his story. But he did mention one more matter he considered important: "You really need to talk with Father John."

Father John McCloskey is the kind of priest who gives liberals the hives, and nightmares as well. He heads the Catholic Information Service in Washington, D.C., and is a priest in the prelature of Opus Dei, a conservative Catholic organization whose very name inspires a blood pressure uptick among liberal critics, who fear its influence and favor within the Vatican. He has a very pleasant speaking voice and appears to write with a razor blade. He is comfortable with controversy and retains a deep and abiding hope in the promises of his faith, even while simultaneously believing that North American Christians, and especially Catholics, can expect to suffer a bloody persecution over the course of the next couple of decades.

Father John is a font of certitude on many cultural and religious subjects, posting his views on his Web site along with articles that are sometimes highly critical of his positions. I sampled a few before our interview, beginning with his views on a subject central to this book.

"The Mainstream Protestants are losing left right and center. They have absolutely no impact." And little remaining pulse. "The upcoming 500th anniversary of the beginning of the Reformation, 1517, will show, I think, that mainstream Protestantism in any culture transforming sense is finished in America. And there is no possibility of a Third or Fourth Great Awakening because secularism and the new paganism in a society sated by undreamt of affluence are not going to lead anyone simply to read the Bible and be converted. America is not a Christian nation in any sense other than that probably a plurality of our fellow citizens have been baptized, although that may change in the decades to come."

We have in some regards already entered a post-Christian era, especially in Europe and North America. "Even though it pains us, it should not surprise us. After all, Christianity has all but disappeared at other times in history, for instance in the Middle East and northern Africa after the invasion of Islam by conquering forces. Now an even more rapid and unsettling de-Christianization is occurring in Europe, through minimal practice of faith in any traditional sense, a collapse of morality based on natural law and the Commandments, and a continental suicide of the native peoples by contraception."

His most stunning—and troubling—thoughts focus on the persecution of North American Christians, which we will take up presently. First, however, I wanted to ask Father John how he pitches Catholic faith to high-profile converts such as Al Regnery, Robert Bork, Robert Novak, and Senator Brownback. Many of his converts—a list that also includes, he said, hundreds of Jews—were well known for their religious skepticism. If Andy Ferguson is correct in saying that joining the church requires intellectual submission, how did Father John persuade so many brilliant people to submit their intellect to a church whose liturgy was formed, for the most part, long before the age of reason and modern science?

When I caught up with John McCloskey, he was on sabbatical in London, writing a book, as it happens, about conversion and evangelizing. He was quick to point out that besides his celebrity catches he has brought many Protestant ministers and Jews into the fold as well, in far greater numbers than reported.

His high-profile converts, he continued, have all shared a "voracious and insatiable appetite for books. I show them the intellectual beauty of the church through the great writings." His authors are mostly but not entirely Catholic and range from Aquinas,

Augustine, and Dante to Philip Hughes, Ronald Knox, G. K. Chesterton, Robert Hugh Benson, C. S. Lewis, T. S. Eliot, Louis Bouyer, Warren Carroll, Orestes Brownson, Russell Shaw, Ken Whitehead, and Cardinal Newman. "Some of these men are themselves converts to Catholicism," Father John said, including Chesterton, several of whose works are on the McCloskey list, including *Orthodoxy* and *The Everlasting Man.* These books show potential converts that conversion is okay. Great minds have crossed over; theirs can too. Certain works appeal to certain minds, he added. Knox's *The Beliefs of Catholics* was important to Robert Bork, while Bernard Nathanson was deeply moved by Stern's *Pillar of Fire.*

Reading, the process by which these men developed their intellects, is also the process by which Father John brought them to submit their intellects to the church. It is subversive, in a sense. Did he agree that conversion requires submission?

Not only that, Father John said. Conversion often entails a costly change in one's personal and public persona. "Many people give up a great deal when they come into the church. Sometimes the cost is in family relations or professional status. Bob Bork was a well-known skeptic and cynic. Bob Novak was the Prince of Darkness. But they found out what Chesterton and other converts discovered. When they submit themselves to the Truth, they find that the Truth has made them free."

While attributing the overall conversion to Grace, Father John credited other factors with helping converts make the leap. One is the presence of good friends, family members, or acquaintances who are already in the church. I mentioned the work of Rodney Stark, who found that most people who take up a new religion do so in large part not because of creed but because of these personal contacts. He called Stark a "great man." He also acknowledged another aid: the prospect of death. "These are intelligent people.

Many of them are older, and they recognize that one day they are going to die. For some of them that day may not be too many years away. So they look around and say that this two-thousand-year-old church must be the real thing."

That is why, he said, he "insists" that those he works with read the history of Catholicism, a point he further elaborates on his Web site. "I do believe the argument, at least rationally, is unassailable—the Catholic Church is true, and no other has ever made a credible claim to be the one that was founded by Him. Either the Lord of History established a church with a visible structure on this earth until He comes again or there is simply no authority that guides and must be obeyed. From the time of the great Schism and the Protestant revolution, the principle of private judgment has given rise to thousands of Christian sects and de-nominations. That is hardly what was intended when He asked His Father 'that all may be one.'"

Conversion has clear benefits. Religious devotion brings a sense of purpose and a measure of peace that elude many nonbe-lievers. Salvation, or at least the promise of such, is no small con-solation. At the same time, Father John indicated, there is a flip side to these benefits. He believed, quite deeply, that Christians are being increasingly marginalized and may face persecution, even unto death, beginning sometime in the next few decades.

This grim scenario is laid out in a Web site essay that tells the story of an old priest addressing a young priest in the year 2030. He starts on a fairly gentle note.

As you may have learned, there were approximately 60 million nominal Catholics at the beginning of the Great Jubilee at the turn of the century. You might ask how we went from that num-ber down to our current 40 million. I guess the answer could be, to put it delicately, consolidation. It is not as bad as it looks. In retrospect it can be seen that only approximately 10% of the sixty or so were "with the program." (Please excuse the anachronism, but I am 77 years old!) I mean to say only 10% of that base assented wholeheartedly to the teaching of the Church and practiced the sacraments in the minimal sense of Sunday Mass and at least yearly confession. The rest, as was inevitable, either left the Church, defected to the culture of death, passed away, or in some cases, at least for a couple of decades, went to various Christian sects, what remained of mainstream Protestantism or Bible Christianity. Since the Catholic birthrate continued to decline among these nominal Catholics and immigration from the Hispanic countries greatly diminished due to stricter governmental policies and better social conditions South of the Border, inevitably the number of Catholics decreased.

That is not the entire story of the decline, however. It is here the tale turns very dark.

In retrospect, the great battles over the last 30 years over the fundamental issues of the sanctity of marriage, the rights of parents, and the sacredness of human life have been of enormous help in renewing the Church and, to some extent, society. We finally received as a gift from God what had been missing from our ecclesial experience these 250 years in North America—a strong persecution that was a true purification for our "sick society." The tens of thousands of martyrs and confessors for the Faith in North America were indeed the "seed of the Church" as they were in pre–Edict of Milan Christianity. The final short and relatively bloodless conflict produced our Regional States of North America. The outcome was by no means an ideal solution but it does allow Christians to live in states that recognize the natural law and divine Revelation, the right of free practice of religion, and laws on marriage, family, and life that reflect the primacy of our Faith. With time and the reality of the ever-decreasing population of the states that worship at the altar of "the culture of death," perhaps we will be able to reunite and fulfill the Founding Fathers of the old United States' dream to be "a shining city on a hill."

I asked Father John if he truly believed persecution and disunion to be a likely possibility. As it happened, the previous day had seen a massive group of pro-choice marchers converging on Washington, D.C., to participate in a rally supporting abortion rights and opposing some Bush administration policies, and indeed the existence of the administration itself.

"After reading about hundreds of thousands marching for death in the nation's capital yesterday, I do believe that there could be serious civil disruption in the years ahead involving violence," he replied. "Simply put, the center cannot hold. There are increasingly two United Stateses that have two irreconcilable ways of looking at and living in the world: one, the culture of life made up of orthodox Christians; the other, the culture of death made up secular practical atheists. One or the other, over time, will win. If the atheists conquer, they will marginalize the Christians to the extent of imprisonment and death. It can happen here. The U.S. is the battleground for the survival of the West. If it goes down, we'll look for a period of dark ages."

I had never heard the term "practical atheists" and asked him what he meant by it.

"In the United States you find few theoretical atheists. But you do find many practical atheists. By that I mean people who may believe in God, and who may even go to church, but God makes no difference in what they otherwise believe and how they live their lives." In a time of conflict, such people cannot be expected to suffer martyrdom or resist the persecution of orthodox Christians.

While the membership roll of the Catholic Church itself is quite impressive—somewhere around 70 million in the United States alone—these numbers may provide a false sense of security. Father John the author agrees totally with his literary creation: "I would say that one in ten Catholics are with the program." They attend Mass regularly, go to Confession, keep the Commandments, and otherwise conform their lives to church teachings. "What does that make the other 90 percent?" I asked. There is a word for people who do not accept the teachings of the Roman Catholic Church, he said. They are called Protestants. And, we can sense, Father John does not think many of them will step forward to rescue the orthodox.

Some weeks after this discussion, Father John posted a new message on the same theme. The United States, he reminded his readers (he was writing from London), is involved in a fierce struggle with the enemies of faith. This is a struggle, he said, "for the soul of our country. This war is more important than the war against Islamic terrorism. Our weapons are, above all, prayer, the sacramental life and our willingness to live the fullness of the Christian life in our family, professional, social and political life."

Nonetheless, he continued, Christians should prepare for the worst. Others, he added, had gone that way before and are much worth emulating.

"St. Thomas More, whose cell in the Tower of London I recently visited, gives us a wonderful example to follow in that regard. His example as a statesman, lawyer and man of letters was outstanding, but his devotion to his family, prayer life and to the Church is even more impressive. It may well be that we or our immediate descendants will lose our heads, but we also could be the ones who bring Catholicism back to the Europe from whence it came to us. Only time will tell."

If there is a bright spot, it is to be found in the Southern Hemisphere. "Already half the Church in the United States is Hispanic," Father John said. "The great challenge for the church is to see that they stay good Catholics and that those who are not good Catholics become good Catholics." Without the Hispanic influx, he added, "we as a nation would be doomed to the almost certain fate of continental Europe: demographic suicide within several decades. The catechesis and evangelization of Hispanic Catholics are therefore crucial for the health of the church and the country." In this he echoes the work of Philip Jenkins, who has reported that the Euro-American Catholics are already in a minority. In Africa, for instance, the number of Catholics has grown from 16 million in the early 1950s to 120 million today, with 228 million expected by 2025. By that year, nearly three-fourths of all Catholics will live in Asia, Latin America, and Africa. Three-quarters of Catholic baptisms take place in Africa, Central and South America, and Asia. "The annual baptism total for the Philippines is higher than the totals for Italy, France, Spain, and Poland combined," Jenkins wrote in the *Atlantic Monthly*.

These Catholics, as Father John would say, are most definitely "with the program."

"The Catholic faith that is rising rapidly in Africa and Asia looks very much like a pre–Vatican II faith, being more traditional in its respect for the power of bishops and priests and in its preference for older devotions," Jenkins concluded. "African Catholicism in particular is far more comfortable with notions of authority and spiritual charisma than with newer ideas of consultation and democracy." In addition, these conservative Catholics will play an increasingly important political role in choosing the church hierarchy. "For thirty years Northern liberals have dreamed of a Third

Vatican Council to complete the revolution launched by Pope John XXIII—one that would usher in a new age of ecclesiastical democracy and lay empowerment. It would be a bitter irony for the liberals if the council were convened but turned out to be a conservative, Southern-dominated affair that imposed moral and theological litmus tests intolerable to North Americans and Europeans—if, in other words, it tried to implement not a new Reformation but a new Counter-Reformation." One senses the unfolding of a liberal nightmare: tens of millions of pre–Vatican II black and brown Catholics in common cause with Robert Novak and Bob Bork.

Not every high-profile Catholic priest is haunted by such a grim vision, though it is important that Father John and his many supporters remain vibrantly orthodox despite the expectation that this could eventually cost them their lives. As we shall see in the next chapter, this attitude puts the lie to the progressive and secular smear that this type of believer is "retreating into orthodoxy." Instead, they believe they may be advancing toward the chopping block.

Father Richard John Neuhaus, formerly a Lutheran, takes a much more hopeful view, at least if one believes that religion does the world more good than harm. In a 2002 speech, he insisted that no secular python endangers the United States or, for that matter, the rest of the world, which he said "is increasingly marked not by secularization but by desecularization." With the exception of Western Europe, he added, "secularization is globally in decline and its supporting worldview—aptly called secularism—is in retreat."

At the same time, Father Neuhaus recognized that American secularists will not fold without a fight and have indeed been quite successful in marginalizing religious observance and especially the role religion plays in public life: "In a usurpation of power that indeed threatens a 'thinly disguised totalitarianism,' the courts have frequently suggested that the separation of church and state means the separation of religion and religiously grounded morality from public life, which means the separation of the deepest convictions of the people from politics, which means the end of democracy and, in fact, the end of politics. Thank God, we are not there yet. But it is the direction in which we in the United States have been moving these last several decades, and it is the real and present danger requiring those of us called conservatives to rally to the defense of the liberal tradition."

American Catholicism, as noted at chapter's start, is hardly the monolithic entity its critics charge. It is the spiritual home of highly motivated liberals, including the writer Garry Wills and socialists too numerous to count. But in its promises and principles, it is a deeply conservative institution and as such will continue to exert its tug on conservatives looking for religious stability and reliability. Conservatives are indeed finding an increasingly warm reception, as evidenced by the growing number of dioceses, now over one hundred, where the old Tridentine Mass is now celebrated. This "Latin Mass," used for some fourteen hundred years prior to the Second Vatican Council, is attracting large numbers of young Catholics, despite its near-invisibility after being replaced in 1970 by the New Order Mass.

The Roman Catholic Church is not the only stronghold of conservative Christianity, of course. The Southern Baptists and evangelicals of various stripes maintain their belief that they are the ones who present the most authentic version of Christianity. Some continue to maintain, not only privately, that the Catholic Church is playing "for the other team," as one non-Catholic put it, a reference to a certain Harlot in the book of Revelation. We will not grope so low for critics, who seem to be in shorter supply these days. That may be because orthodox Christians both Protestant and Catholic, and of course Orthodox, are increasingly willing to overlook differences and focus on beliefs and causes they hold in common.

One criticism of the Catholic Church that is worth a closer look comes from the Orthodox Church, which argues that Orthodoxy, not Catholicism, is the closest thing to true Christianity we are likely to find in our time. Some conservatives consider Orthodoxy to be the true castle keep of the faith. It seems safe to assume, in any case, that most Americans, conservative or otherwise, have little firsthand knowledge of this church, which has taken in thousands of mainline refugees, including a large number of Episcopal priests. I knew of one such priest and his wife, both of whom found themselves too Protestant to make the journey to Rome but eventually discovered that the road to Byzantium took them to their spiritual promised land. This couple live outside of Baltimore, though their church truly does transport them to another time and another place, both far, far away from that old port town.

Five

The Orthodox Church

Some Roads Lead to Byzantium

You know you're in the presence of truly traditional religion when your hostess greets you at the door, invites you inside, and quickly directs your attention to the family relic.

Frederica Mathewes-Green welcomed me to her Baltimore-area home and ushered me to a small, candlelit portion of the front room. Here hung several small icons and also, she pointed out, a relic. "A relic?" I said, with some surprise, adding that when I think of relics I think of such things as fingers, toes, ears, and whatever else might be snipped from a revered corpse. Frederica responded with a vigorous bit of head nodding and to my surprise told me I was correct. Their relic, she explained, is a chip from the foot of Rafael Hawaweeny, a former Orthodox bishop of Brooklyn. It was contained in a small thin case that could easily be mistaken for an elaborate greeting card.

"So that's really a piece of Bishop Hawaweeny?" I asked. Frederica nodded again. She was not ashamed. Quite the contrary. She said that not all relics are body pieces. The Shroud of Turin is a relic. But the word *relic* does tend to bring to mind body parts and an expectation—perhaps strongly encouraged by the vendor—that it will bestow blessings and perhaps facilitate the working of miracles. She knows all this, and knows how outsiders are likely to react, and she is quite comfortable with her expectations and her visitor's apparent skepticism. She is an Orthodox believer, and radiant in her faith.

It has not always been so. Frederica and her husband Gary are very much refugees from the mainline. Their story is more poignant than most. Gary was for many years an Episcopal priest. Both were strongly dedicated to their denomination and had worked long and hard toward its rescue and rejuvenation. When it came time to leave, Frederica's heart was broken. Tears were shed. The denomination that had drawn her from Eastern religion into Christianity, and that she assumed would be the church that buried her and her children as well, had betrayed her trust and her hopes.

But there's a bright side to their story as well. Her greatest regret is that she and Gary did not find Orthodoxy earlier.

Frederica Mathewes-Green is well known to conservatives as a writer and speaker with a passionate interest in the pro-life position. She is in her early fifties, somewhat petite, with gray streaking her thick mane of brown hair. She smiles a great deal and nods as questions are asked. I sensed that she was attempting to discern what my assumptions and motives might be as much as she was listening to my questions. Orthodox believers have reason to be on their guard. They are little known and less understood, at least in the United States. Their ways are most definitely not the ways of the Methodists and Presbyterians.

Like many if not most Americans, I knew of the Orthodox Church but knew very little about it. I had heard that the Orthodox service can be quite different from the basic Protestant service, that it is deeply and uniquely mysterious, the type of service that Dean Kelley would agree is central to organizational success and also attractive to traditionalist believers. As I was to find, some of their beliefs are indeed deeply mystical, by generous description. The Orthodox also have serious disagreements with Western Christianity and hold that some of Christianity's finest minds—

Augustine, for example—were not so fine after all. They also believe the Catholic Church stepped out of line back in the eleventh
century, and as such is not the true church but a renegade of sorts.

We would get to all that. But first I wanted to know why Frederica and Gary had fled the Episcopal Church and why they had
decided on Orthodoxy.

At the beginning of Frederica's religious journey there was
Rome. "I was raised a nominal Catholic in Charleston, South Carolina," said Frederica. "My faith pretty much died when I was
fourteen." By college years she had become interested in Hinduism. "It was the most colorful of the Eastern religions." Gary,
also from Charleston, had been an atheist in college but experienced the subtle beginning of a religious awakening while reading
the Gospel of Mark. "There was something about Jesus," he concluded. Jesus spoke with an authority that reached across the centuries. And so Gary began studies at an Episcopal seminary in
northern Virginia. Frederica began seminary studies as well, though
she admits to being motivated by a more mundane desire: going to
seminary and reading about God seemed a far better way to spend
her days than getting a job.

Yet a Christian seed had been planted. During a visit to Dublin
its first shoots broke through. As Frederica gazed at a statue of Jesus she was suddenly "struck to my knees," she explained. Simultaneously she heard a voice (an interior voice, she added, though of
unknown origin) tell her, "I am your life." This was not the stuff of
Hinduism. This was straight out of ancient Palestine. A Damascus
Road event, she said.

Gary's faith was deepening at a more measured pace. There
were no dramatic events to match Frederica's. He came around to
her position through study and contemplation. After completing
seminary, he was ordained an Episcopal priest. This was 1977.
There was joy and a sense of purpose, but also a sense of fore-

boding. Gary and Frederica knew that their church faced serious challenges, most from within. It was not simply the matter of media-savvy bishops preaching the Unrisen Jesus. The denomination seemed to be brimming with priests who thought the celebrity heretics might have come across the real truth of the Christian matter. Their cause was far advanced, perhaps unstoppable.

At the same time, Gary and Frederica felt they had been "called" to the Episcopal Church. They had to do what they could to preserve and, with any luck, advance its traditions. They were hopeful, but not unreasonably so. The church, they concluded, would either be brought back to its senses within a decade or be lost forever. Restoring it to orthodoxy would, they both believed, require direct intervention from the Holy Spirit.

Accordingly, Gary and Frederica believed the church's hope lay in the charismatic movement, with which they were both involved. "We had a saying that the Episcopal Church would be either charismatic or dead in ten years," Frederica said. They had some reason for confidence. They had seen the Spirit work marvelous wonders.

During a gathering of charismatics at Catholic University, Frederica said, a young man had suddenly stood up and admitted that he and several friends had murdered someone the night before. "There was a moment of silence," Frederica recalled, but then "a great peace came down on us. Someone else stood up and said he wanted to pray for this man. We sang a hymn. Someone else got up and prayed for him. I was so impressed that this group had the resources to deal with something so bizarre." The Holy Spirit was given credit, and it was hoped that the same Spirit would help save their errant denomination.

But as the months passed Frederica's interest in the charismatic movement began to fade. "I started to burn out," she said. "I became very weary of what increasingly seemed like a shallow kind of emotionalism. I would go to a women's retreat, and everyone had their arms in the air, praying in tongues. More and more, I wanted silence. I had a sense that there was an oil lamp within me, and I wanted the silence to sit and contemplate that inner flame."

There was another problem as well: politics. Gary had trans-ferred from a Virginia church to a new church in Ellicott City, Maryland. This was not many miles away on the map but in a dif-ferent world theologically. "The Episcopal Church had been going leftist long before our move," Gary said, "but overall it was fairly moderate and we thought we could hang in there." Maryland changed all that.

"There were two parishes in Ellicott City," Gary explained. His church maintained a high, Anglo-Catholic tradition. "Down the street, they had Jack Spong in for a week of lectures." Spong, as noted earlier, had greatly distanced himself from traditional Christian teachings. He was also perhaps the most famous Episco-pal bishop in the world. He drew well—so well as to suggest that perhaps his views were the future of the church. "I had to ask my-self a question," Gary said. "How can you have two churches that are this different operating in the same communion?" He and Frederica believed the denomination should be consistent in its teachings. There were souls at stake—including those belonging to their children.

"I was becoming afraid that by the time they became adoles-cents, the Episcopal Church would no longer be a faithful church," Frederica said. Gary could offer no reassurance. He was finding it increasingly difficult to determine exactly what the Episcopal posi-tion was on key theological and moral issues. It seemed there were no longer any fixed positions.

One small bit of hope remained. Gary and Frederica enter-tained the idea that grassroots rebellion of sorts might rally traditionalist priests and faithful laypeople. In 1991 Gary and five other traditionalist priests composed what came to be known as the Baltimore Declaration, which asserted seven points of orthodoxy regarding the Resurrection, Virgin Birth, and other fundamentals of the faith. They printed up one thousand copies. Frederica and Al Kimel, one of the declaration's authors, took copies to the church's General Convention, held that year in Phoenix. Surely, they thought, some priests would step forward to support the declaration, and from that small spark might come a purifying fire. They distributed the declaration to convention participants. They waited. And waited. They waited in vain. There was no response. All that had been accomplished, Frederica and Gary concluded, was that they had revealed themselves as being irrevocably out of step with the modern Episcopal Church.

That point was made indelible when a resolution was put forward calling for the Episcopal clergy to abstain from sex outside of marriage. This would not appear to be an unreasonable demand. It was fully in keeping with the denomination's traditional teachings on sex and family life. Yet the resolution failed. "There was no turning back after that," said Frederica, who said the resolution's defeat brought her to tears. Gary knew departure time had arrived.

"It took me a while to realize the problem wasn't Jack Spong," Gary said. "The problem is that the bishops had no power to do anything about the Spongs. And it was clear that the church had come to agree with Bishop Pike that there was really no such thing as heresy." He was not alone in this belief. Gary met with several church leaders who "were much higher up than I was, and I believed they could see further and clearer into the future of the church. I asked them where they thought the church would be in ten years. To a man, they all had negative appraisals." Gary, who has dark hair and a beard, shook his head as he spoke, in contrast to Frederica's nodding. It was as if he still could not believe what had happened to his church.

I asked how the liberal wing responded to declining membership. Didn't this indicate that they were taking the denomination into oblivion?

"Any sane person," Gary replied, "would agree that you've got problems if you're losing a great portion of your church population. But the liberal priests would actually say it was a good thing. They said [that] 'what we're losing are the peripheral believers,' and that shedding all those people would actually make the church stronger. Some actually believed the church was not liberal enough."

While their future was clearly no longer with the Episcopal Church, leaving was not easy. Gary's entire career had been with the denomination. He would have to find another job. Frederica had come to the church from Hinduism. This was not a divorce to be taken lightly. "We believed we had been called to the Episcopal Church," Frederica said, "and we struggled with our belief that even if the Episcopal Church was lost to apostasy, there might be a role for us still. I used to say to Gary, 'Didn't God need chaplains on the *Titanic*? Hadn't we better stay where he planted us?'"

Gary mulled his options, including Rome. The Catholic Church had taken in many priests fleeing the mainline. Gary, however, did not experience that tug. His reading of history had persuaded him that Rome's claims to be the "true church" were not convincing. He was especially wary of the papacy, which he had studied with morbid fascination. There were other hurdles that could not be cleared, especially "traces of salvation-by-works in Catholic practice."

But there was another option he had been considering. The Orthodox Church was also harvesting refugees from the mainline, and there was much in this church to appeal to Gary. It had a beautiful liturgy that appeared to be beyond political manipulation. The faithful not only could know where the church stood on theological issues but had every confidence these positions would not be adjusted or abandoned at the behest of pressure groups. The church had also developed a "fast-track" process to bring dissenting priests into its fold. Gary was invited to join a small group of disaffected Protestant clergymen meeting under the auspices of Orthodox evangelist Father Peter Gillquist. Orthodoxy, he soon learned, had taken in thousands of Protestant refugees. In 1987 some two thousand conservative believers, including many clergy members, had participated in a mass conversion service. "About half the clergy are converts," Gary said. "About 30 percent of those are former Episcopalians."

Gary finally had an answer to Frederica's *Titanic* metaphor: "You know what God needed on the *Titanic*? Lifeboats. We know where there's a ship that doesn't sink. Let's try to get as many people to safety as possible."

And so the Episcopal Church lost one more priest, and a deeply committed priest's wife and family. Gary went through the fast-track process and was posted to a small Orthodox Church some ten miles from his final Episcopal posting. He is known to his flock as Father Gregory. And both he and Frederica say they wish they had found Orthodoxy earlier.

I asked Frederica why she feels so strongly about her new faith. Politics aside, how is the faith itself different from her Episcopal experience?

One significant difference, she replied, is what Orthodoxy requires of its members. "Mainline churches demand nothing," she said. "There's no vigor there. Orthodoxy flows through your entire life." I happened to be visiting during Lent, a time during which a pious Episcopalian might give up ice cream, or in extreme cases midweek golf. In the Orthodox home, Lent is taken much more seriously. The soul is nourished, and the stomach denied. No meat, fish, or dairy is to be consumed during these forty-odd days. Alcohol and olive oil are forbidden during the week. Families are forever in church.

I asked about theological differences. What about the break with the Roman church?

Orthodoxy, she explained, holds that the Roman church splintered Christianity when it took upon itself the task of adding the word *filioque* ("and the Son") to the Nicene Creed. "In an effort to elevate the second person of the Trinity," Frederica has written in an account of her conversion,

> it dilutes the singular authority of the Father, and changes the Trinity from—visually speaking—a triangle with God the Father at the top, to one tipped over, both Father and Son above the Spirit. Orthodoxy is indeed "patri-archal," that is, the Father (the pater) is the arche, the source and font of all. In Orthodoxy, it's not Jesus, but the Father whom those serving at the altar represent, and whatever else a woman can be (and, in Orthodoxy, she can be anything else: choir director, lector, teacher, head of the parish council) she cannot be a Father. She can be a Mother, of course, and so there is a recognized and honored role for the priest's wife, with a title: Khouria (Arabic), Matushka (Russian), or Presbytera (Greek).

This split occurred on Christmas Day 1054, which reminds us, among other things, that the Orthodox have long memories and exacting standards. This is not a "whatever" organization, as in "Is the Holy Ghost a real being or merely a symbol?—Whatever."

Orthodoxy also takes great pride in its uniqueness and its reverence for mystery. "An Orthodox theologian said that Catholicism is an institution with Sacred Mysteries [sacraments]," Frederica said, "and Orthodoxy is a Sacred Mystery with an institution. This goes along with rejecting the papacy. We reject the idea of that kind of top-down leadership; we believe in the faith that grows up from the grass roots. They are museum guards, not museum curators." Orthodoxy departs from Western Christianity in other areas as well. "We don't have the body-soul split Augustine introduced to the Western church," she said, and Orthodoxy rejects the doctrine of original sin. Do they believe a reunion between Orthodoxy and Roman Catholicism is possible? Gary said the Roman church will be welcomed back into the fold once it puts aside its theological innovations and acknowledges that it is "first among equals"—but no more than that.

Gary and Frederica have found their spiritual rock and built their house upon it. "This was a church that can never apostatize," Gary said as he donned his black cassock and prepared to depart for Lenten vespers. There is no mechanism, he explained, by which interested parties could even begin to introduce the liberalism that has devastated his former church. "I don't think the Episcopal Church will totally disappear," he concluded. "There are still people who like the idea of being Episcopalian. It's still a strong brand." And so he departed to present the ancient message.

Frederica asked if I had ever attended an Orthodox service. I told her of my plans to do so. The Orthodox service, she advised, is not to be confused with what I had encountered in my life as an itinerant Presbyterian. When you worship with the Orthodox, she said, you enter another world.

Before entering that world, I took a whirlwind tour of church history with the help of Timothy Ware (known to the faithful as Bishop Kallistos of Diokleia), a prominent church historian. Orthodoxy, Ware writes in *The Orthodox Church* (1997), is a sprawl-

ing entity encompassing all the churches that make up Oriental
Orthodoxy and Eastern Orthodoxy, the latter being in communion with the Patriarch of Constantinople. When we refer to the
Orthodox Church, Ware says, we are talking about the Eastern
Orthodox Church, which comprises thirteen self-governing,
or "autocephalous," churches, including the four ancient Patri-
archates of Constantinople, Alexandria, Antioch, and Jerusalem;
nine other autocephalous churches, including the well-known
Russian and Greek churches; and a small handful of "autonomous"
churches. There are over 200 million baptized members, Ware
writes, though a sizable portion of those may not be regular practitioners.

Orthodoxy has known great challenges throughout its history,
including clashes with mobilized Islam and, in modern times, a
devastating testing by communism. Between 1914 and the start of
World War II, Ware writes, Orthodoxy was reduced from 54,174
churches and 51,105 priests and deacons to a few hundred churches
and priests. There was a wartime thaw, but persecution resumed
under Nikita Khrushchev and continued, at varying levels of in-
tensity, into the age of Mikhail Gorbachev. Today Orthodox believers celebrate many martyrs from the Communist era. The
church must also live with the painful knowledge that many Russian Orthodox officials collaborated with the Soviet government.
The opening of KGB files in 1992 produced devastating revela-
tions, Ware admits: "Many of the laity have been scandalized to
discover the extent of the collaboration under communism between certain bishops and the secret police." The church's persecution of Eastern Rite Catholics was another scandal. The Greek
Catholic Church had been forcefully incorporated into the Orthodox Church in 1946, and most of its bishops died in captivity. The
authorities of the Moscow Patriarchate collaborated with the gov-

ernment in this persecution. Ware believes that to be his church's darkest hour.

No institution escapes corruption, and this church is no exception. But I had heard that the Orthodox Church is exceptional in its ability to create a sense of otherworldliness in its worship services, thus transporting believers to a place where, Scripture tells us, corruption has no hold. My first experience with Orthodox worship was literary. A short essay on composer Igor Stravinsky (1882–1971), who returned to Orthodoxy in his forties, offered a striking example of the powerful effect these services have on devoted believers. Immediately upon entering his church, the essay notes, Stravinsky prostrated himself on the floor before the altar and prayed—for two full hours. That accomplished, Stravinsky rose, received the Sacrament, and then resumed prayer, this time with his head touching the stone floor. This is something you won't see in a Presbyterian church, and it serves as a reminder that the Being worshiped at Orthodox services is not the one who walked in on two legs, as was the case with our visit to First Unitarian.

Frederica had explained that in their small stone church worshipers stand throughout the service, at least if they are able, and that services can easily go on over an hour and a half. They had no musical instruments, she added. She also said that I should be aware that inside every Orthodox altar there resides a relic. Her message seemed to be that God's house, Orthodox version, is quite different from my house.

That I found to be quite true.

A standard-issue mainliner will first notice the smell of incense, a subtle difference but a signal that the visitor has entered a different environment, one that perhaps smells much like the environment of Christian services a thousand years ago. The visitor will also notice a musical difference. In some churches there are no instruments, simply a choir singing a mesmerizing collection of ancient chants and modes. Other churches might use an organ, but "Ode to Joy" is not in the repertoire.

At the front of the church is a large wall covered with often-brilliant painted icons. This is called the iconostasis. This wall is breached by several doors: a double door in the middle, called the Royal Doors, and doors to the left and right, called the Angel Doors or Deacon's Doors. These side doors are used mainly by the altar boys and deacons, while the Royal Doors are used for higher purposes, as when the priest brings in the Sacrament. There is a great deal of movement in the service: a great drama is being played out. The priest sings much of the liturgy, making generous use of the minor scales. He is sometimes joined by the choir. Some portions are done in Greek; there is no equivalent of the "children's message" presented in some Protestant churches, typically delivered in Barneyese, which inspires some adults (ahem) to seriously eye the exits.

These differences add up to a profound departure from the typical mainline environment. There is another difference as well, one even more profound. Sooner or later the feet begin to hurt, especially when one is visiting a church without pews. (Some Orthodox churches do have pews, though worshipers are called to their feet continually and sometimes must stay there for long stretches.) Soon thereafter the knees and legs may stiffen as well. We are losing contact with our comfort zone and may begin to long for the relative comfort of a hard wooden pew. There's a benefit to this, my psychotherapist wife suggests. The presence of pain can assist the process of cognition. Pain is also a universal human experience, and central to the Christian message.

There is also the knowledge that in the altar there rests a relic. This knowledge, for some visitors at least, casts an especially strange and mysterious aura over a church service. Ours is not a society that lives easily with death. Ours is a society with many members who fear so much as buttering an ear of corn lest it hasten the day of demise. Having a piece of a dead person in the altar radiates several messages, the most profound perhaps being that such is the way of all flesh, no matter how much fat you cut from your diet.

The presence of relics also returns worshipers to an earlier era. The historian Paul Johnson tells us that Archbishop Albert of Mainz had some nine thousand relics in his sixteenth-century collection, including "whole bodies of saints, a bone of Isaac, manna from the wilderness, a bit of Moses's burning bush, a jar from Cana (with actual wine in it), a bit of the crown of thorns, and one of the stones that killed St. Stephen." Another collection, held in the Lateran basilica, included the heads of both Peter and Paul, along with "the Ark of the Covenant, the Tablets of Moses, the Rod of Aaron, an urn of manna, the Virgin's tunic, John the Baptist's hair shirt, the five loaves and two fishes from the Feeding of the Five Thousand and the dining table used at the Last Supper. The nearby chapel of St. Lawrence," Johnson concludes, "boasted the foreskin and umbilical cord of Christ, preserved in a gold and jeweled crucifix filled with oil."

Frederica Mathewes-Green points out that the relics in her church are quite humble by comparison. They are brought into the church during the consecration process. "A church can't be consecrated until all its bills are paid off," she explained. "There can't be a mortgage on the church. But once it is paid off, the bishop comes and performs the elaborate consecration service," which includes the installation of relics. "In our case, the relics were embedded in beeswax and wrapped in aluminum foil, so that if necessary they could be recovered." She acknowledged that the presence of relics "naturally sounds bizarre to modern Christians." Their purpose, she said, is to remind the faithful that Orthodoxy resists "Gnosticism and neo-Platonism, which has always troubled Christians in its insistence that body is bad, spirit is good." When one comes into proper relationship with God, Frederica added, "material creation is shot through with God's presence." Relics represent the presence of God even in the dead and remind the faithful of the transformation that ensures everlasting life. An interesting afterlife for a chip of bone from a dead man's foot. "There's a saying in the Orthodox Church," Frederica summed up. "The purpose of our church is to make relics. We are an incarnational faith. In our tradition, the body is as much a bearer of the presence of God as the soul. It too is transformed by God's presence."

The Orthodox service, with its incense, icons, chanting, candlelight, flesh in the altar, and small dose of physical pain, creates an aura of mystery and otherworldliness unmatched in the mainline. This is not an extension of one's den. During one Orthodox service this itinerant Presbyterian recalled his annoyance at having to rise to sing the final hymn. Similarly, as Orthodox prayer stretched on, seemingly into Monday, it came to mind how finely tuned and timed mainline services tend to be: welcome, announcements, opening hymn, minute for missions, children's story, offering, first Scripture reading, hymn, prayer, second reading, sermon, final hymn, benediction, NFL. Mainline sermon topics vary, but a popular theme is what God can do for us if we will let Him. He is often said to desire forming a partnership to help us realize our dreams. Operators are standing by. . . . If the message somehow takes us too close to noon, a verse may be cut from the final hymn. As the benediction is given, the back pews begin to empty; as minister and assistants stroll down the aisle, one hears the sound of engines starting in the parking lot. It is all very orderly, like a business meeting or a precise dose of medicine.

Othodoxy, by contrast, is not for everyone. Many believers will find it far too mysterious, too otherworldly, too time-consuming. Some Orthodox beliefs are unusual, by generous standards. "Orthodox still expect miracles," Frederica told me, including "biolocation" and levitation. "We do have instances where people do what we call 'soul-reading' in which they can look at you and tell you your history." At the same time, the uniqueness of the worship service—which in Frederica's words "plugs you into the first century" and at any rate takes us far from the twenty-first—makes it a serious option for serious believers.

This church also serves as an antidote to the sneering charge that traditionalists "flee into orthodoxy" as if orthodoxy (or Orthodoxy) is a summer camp.

Orthodox Christians, whatever their affiliation, have set themselves a demanding path. They have put themselves at odds with many of the central tenets of modern life. They reject the cult of the autonomous, unencumbered self. They profess a belief in sin, and especially sexual sin, which wins them little admiration. The Orthodox Christians submit themselves to a God who is stern in His ways and harsh in His judgments, a God to which they will be accountable one fearful day. This is no 30 percent deity. He has counted every hair on every head and is keeping tabs of every thought and action.

He is a great and perplexing mystery. He brought man into being for reasons unfathomable, and with the full knowledge of what would befall this creature made in His image. There would be endless calamity, murder, and proud disbelief. Man's children would die by the thousands each day, and legions would curse His name and reject His greatest offering, His Son, who would suffer to an unimaginable degree on their behalf. Every trial and tear was known at the foundation of time, and still He created, and still He came.

This is a serious God. This is not a lodge brother. This is why Stravinsky prayed with his head to the stones.

Christian orthodoxy is not a retreat into the easy life. That much better describes the Unitarian way and the demand-free

Episcopal Church. But while orthodox (and Orthodox) Christianity is rigorous, it is increasingly popular. Because of its uniquely mysterious and otherworldly nature, Orthodoxy can expect to attract increasing numbers of Americans in flight from the mainline. Other churches that promote Christian orthodoxy, though of a different type, are also doing well, including those associated with the Southern Baptist Convention (SBC), which was my next stop.

The SBC is made up of autonomous Southern Baptist churches that have banded together to preserve their Bible-based faith. This is not a liturgical church. As we saw in chapter 3, Baptist ministers are more likely to have a "biblical" worldview than any other members of the Protestant clergy. There's a good reason for that. In the view of the Southern Baptist Convention, the Bible is without error. Inerrancy is taught in Southern Baptist seminaries.

Dr. Albert Mohler and Dr. Richard Land, whom I was off to see, both teach at the Southern Baptist Theological Seminary in Louisville, Kentucky. They teach Adam and Eve, Noah's Ark, and the Risen Christ. And like other Baptists, they have contemporary interests as well. The SBC teaches that modern-day wives should "submit" to their husbands and that the faithful should pray for the conversion of Jews. And many Southern Baptists, including Mohler and Land, hope, pray, and believe that in the near future an alliance of orthodox believers will rock the secular world to its foundations. They are hard at work to undermine if not destroy some of its central dogmas, including *Roe v. Wade*.

Mohler and Land have another lesson to teach as well. The Southern Baptist Convention has not always welcomed orthodox Christianity. In many respects it was going the way of the Protestant mainline. It drew quite close to the precipice, according to many of its conservative members. By the dictates of conventional wisdom, it was doomed to become irrevocably liberal. For the conventional wisdom holds that once an institution goes liberal, there is no turning back.

The Southern Baptist conservatives, however, had no use for conventional wisdom. They have one Book and launched a counterrevolution on its behalf. They won, and they took no prisoners. Conservatives in other liberal-besieged denominations may find their story instructive.

Six

The Southern Baptists

Some Roads Lead to Louisville

Once an organization goes liberal, it will stay liberal. So it is written in the political playbook, and religious denominations are said to be no different from the foundations, companies, and educational institutions that have gone left, never to return.

Yet when conservatives in the Southern Baptist Convention concluded that liberals were taking their organization the way of the mainline, they took a different page from the political playbook: they conducted a purge. Their battle cry was not explicitly about sex, as it has been, lately at least, throughout the mainline. Instead, it was summed up in two words: biblical inerrancy. The Bible, the conservatives insisted, is right in all that it teaches and affirms. Put another way: don't mess with the Text.

The conservatives' belief that their denomination's future lay in the biblical past has paid off. The Southern Baptist Convention is the largest non-Catholic Christian group in the United States. It continues to attract mainline refugees and believers seeking traditional Christianity. In addition, the SBC provides many foot soldiers and generals in the culture wars, which the latter, as we shall see, do not believe will have been fought in vain.

The belief in inerrancy puts Southern Baptists at odds with many Christians, including other Baptists. There are around fifty different types of Baptists, including those who handle vipers, congregations of messianic Jews, earth worshipers, longtime advocates of gay marriage, and adherents of other positions traditionalists reject. Southern Baptists are the largest group; their churches are autonomous and speak corporately as the Southern Baptist Convention. There are some 16 million Southern Baptists, and counting.

Southern Baptists live by a strict code (in theory, at least). They tend to forswear swearing, tobacco, and wine. They do not blink when asked what they believe: Virgin Birth? Yes. Walk on water? Of course. Bodily resurrection? Absolutely. Second Coming? You can count on it. They are feared by progressives, with some reason. The Southern Baptists are sending large numbers of their young through conservative seminaries, from which they are posted across America and the world. They will not likely stray from their inerrant message or their cultural conservatism. But it is not true, as the progressives would have it, that Baptists are typically slow of mind, slack of jaw, and animated by prejudice. Nor is the SBC led by unintelligent people. One of their instructors, Dr. Richard Land, whom I was off to meet, went to Oxford with Bill Clinton, from whom he distinguishes himself in several ways, including, he says, "the fact that I am the only one of us who graduated." The other, Dr. Albert Mohler, is also brilliant. What is also striking about these two Southern Baptists is how different they are in temperament and outlook, despite their common theological and political beliefs. To know one Southern Baptist is not to know all Southern Baptists.

Southern Baptist Theological Seminary, located in Louisville, Kentucky, is not so far from St. John's Church in Richmond—six hundred miles or so, on the other side of West Virginia, where the Pentecostals keep the home fires burning. It is only a mile or so from the Louisville Presbyterian Theological Seminary, though the Baptists inhabit vastly different spiritual territory. The Baptist world includes Noah's Ark, Jonah's whale, stone tablets inscribed by the finger of God, a burning bush, an active Devil, and a talking serpent. Jesus was born of the Virgin Mary, walked on water, raised the dead, was crucified at the demand of the Sanhedrin, and rose after three days—in bodily form, with a hole in his side. He now sits at His Father's right hand, where both shall judge the quick and the dead. Which from the Southern Baptist perspective is very bad news for liberal Episcopalians.

Southern is one of six Southern Baptist seminaries, whose total enrollment has risen 8 percent a year over the past several years and closes in on 15,000. Southern enrolls 3,600 students, mostly white men. Its buildings are made of brick, and the campus has an open feel to it. Students do not wear suits and ties, as some might expect. Some couples walk about hand in hand. These are mixed-sex couples. Homosexuality still counts as a sin here. There is no gay student union. Nor is there a student pub. Overnight visitors stay at the Legacy Center and are asked not to smoke. There's no mention of drinking; one assumes that is not believed necessary.

Southern vibrates with evangelical commitment. A hallway in the student activities center bore a large world map highlighting sites of ongoing Christian persecution; further down the hall toward the cafeteria flyers sought missionaries willing to work in southeast Africa—and Alabama. A "Global Prayergram" asked devotional support for struggling believers in Suriname, Algeria, Morocco, China, the Czech Republic, and dozens more places around the globe. Religious reminders were also found in the gym. In the workout room a large picture of a western butte bore this message: "A pile of rocks ceases to be a rock pile when somebody contemplates it with the idea of a cathedral in mind." There is also a warning from Saint Paul to not take physical exercise too seriously. One exerciser worked at a laptop between repetitions. The students tend to be friendly and outgoing. Several said hello to me as we passed in the hallway, just as several waved at me as I drove around campus. Here and there one does, however, encounter a budding Kierkegaard, lost in thought, eyes intensely penetrating the veil of illusion.

Though Baptists are rumored to avoid books at all costs (save for the Book), that is not the impression a visitor is likely to take home from Southern. A display in the library foyer suggested several works, including Carl F. H. Henry's *The Uneasy Conscience of Modern Fundamentalism* (1947), which encourages evangelicals to maintain their allegiance to biblical "fundamentals" while engaging the secular culture. Richard Weaver's *Ideas Have Consequences*, standard bedside reading for conservative activists, was also recommended, along with a book titled *Nine Marks of a Healthy Church* and a CD titled *Old Regular Baptist*, whose cover features an old photograph of three people standing in a river. There was also a signed copy of Robert Frost's *A Masque of Reason*. In the bookstore one finds many titles perhaps not available at the seminary down the road. A shelf of current bestsellers included several books about the End Times: *Unveiling the End Time in Our Time*, *Babylon Rising*, *Armageddon*, and *Soon: The Beginning of the End*. There were books about the power of *The Praying Woman*, *The Praying Parent*, and *The Praying Husband*. A bit deeper into the store one finds Milton, Virgil, Boswell, Cervantes, Swift, Plato, Aristotle—and some writers who might find it amusing that their work is being sold to Baptist youth, including David Hume, Machiavelli, and Mark Twain, whose views of biblical inerrancy were distinctly different from the SBC position. "It is full of interest," he wrote of the Bible in his *Letters from the Earth*. "It has noble poetry in it; and some clever fables; and some blood-drenched history; and some good morals; and a wealth of obscenity; and upwards of a thousand lies." The presence of Twain and Hume would indicate that Southern Baptists are more open-minded than given credit for. There are a few other reminders of the outside world as well. Around noon the small chapel in the student activities building was empty, but in the lounge a dozen or so students listened to Gloria Allred prattling on Fox News about the latest celebrity sexual assault case. Thankfully, the time had come for my interview with Southern's president, R. Albert Mohler.

Dr. Mohler welcomed me to his office warmly; I had interviewed him a few years previously and had apparently not caused fatal offense. As before, he appeared energetic and youthful (he was born in 1959), though one quickly detects an inner seriousness and sternness. In his dark suit he looked something like a banker, though not one who lends money easily. A thundercloud also came to mind.

So, I began, how about those Episcopalians?

The consecration of Gene Robinson "is a tragic act of intentional apostasy," Mohler began. "The Episcopal Church has turned its back on the authority of Scripture and its own traditions. It is so inclusive it no longer defines itself according to Scripture. It is so politically correct that it is not concerned about heresy, and so tolerant it can't tolerate the truth of the Truth. The Episcopal Church has sold its soul to the spirit of the age."

If Mohler sounds like a well-rehearsed pundit, it is because he is a well-rehearsed pundit. He writes a daily column for Cross-walk.com and hosts a daily radio show with national reach. Twenty percent of his listeners, he said, are truckers, many of whom call in with messages of support. He is also an ordained minister and professor of Christian theology at Southern.

The current troubles, he quickly added, did not begin with Gene Robinson. "The theological problems in the Anglican Communion go back to the nineteenth century," Mohler continued. "The

Church of England never met the post-Enlightenment challenges to Christian Truth." As a result, "the early twentieth century was the spawning ground for the social revolution we are living through today. The flappers put to death the last vestiges of Victorian heritage. The sense of moral absolutes vanished among writers, academics, and philosophers. We entered an era that was avowedly secular. Sex became merely another type of self-expression."

The mention of flappers and sex brought to mind another bit of the Baptist caricature: it is widely believed that a conversation about sex with a Baptist, and especially a Baptist minister, is bound to be brief. Not so. Mohler can talk sex all day and into the night. By his reading, sex has been a primary solvent of traditional Christianity and social cohesion. Contraception and abortion, for instance, "decoupled sex from marriage and procreation." Sexual exclusivity—one man, one woman, together for life—thus gave way to "profligacy, widespread adultery, and divorce," all of which lost their stigma. Homosexuality is getting the same treatment. "It took a while for so-called middle-class morality to give way, but when it did, homosexuality advanced with lightning speed," said Mohler. "We are left with two choices. We can either live by the biblical morality of sex or live in a state of sexual anarchy."

Mohler sounds much like a conservative Catholic. His attitude reminded me of postings on Father John McCloskey's Web site. This brought to mind yet another aspect of the caricature: that Southern Baptists are, by virtue of their high growth rate, triumphalist. Mohler is anything but triumphalist. Indeed, as our conversation continued he often appeared to be a man with very little hope.

Marriage, for instance, is a subject that brings out his darkest forebodings. Marriage, Mohler said, has traditionally been the firewall between anarchy and order, but by now it has been battered to the point of collapse. "Christian marriage is a radical notion. It tells man and wife to be faithful to each other until death. It creates gifts of accountability. And it insists that nonmarried people keep their pants on." That is the short version of the Southern Baptist cultural catechism: keep your pants on.

Unfortunately, Mohler said, the concept of sexual restraint is not widely admired, even among many members of the Christian clergy. Liberal churches, he said, "make no demands, including demands on sexual behavior. Why should, for example, a sixteen-year-old boy and girl bother to go to a liberal church? What does this church have to offer that's any different from what they get from the culture? The church tells them that if they want, they can have sex. They already know that. That's what the society tells them. The church needs to tell them that they can't have sex, and has to explain why."

That's not likely, he added. "The mainline denominations have decided that the most basic human drive, sex, can be permanently separated from the most basic human institution, marriage. There is no room for Christianity in that equation." But there is room for much else. "It's unlikely same-sex marriage can be stopped, and after that we will be debating, at the very least, polygamy and group marriages."

I suggested to Mohler that he seemed very grim, even grimmer than when we had met a few years before. Could he find no reason for hope?

Yes, he said with a slight smile, there have been a few positive developments. "The students on this campus are not only more conservative than their parents," he said, "but they are more conservative than their grandparents." They were also more committed to the faith than either parents or grandparents.

I said I found that surprising. Many do, after all, come from Baptist families.

"There is no longer any social value in saying you're a Christian," Mohler replied. "These students' parents and grandparents came up in a time when Christianity was a social convention. The same was true of marriage. For their grandparents, marriage was culturally and socially acceptable, and divorce and adultery were bad. Homosexuality was off the radar screen. But their parents, the boomers, threw out sexual morality. They grew up and got married, which made them a little more conservative, but they also engaged in serial divorce. And so the boomers' children—the students who are now on our campus—were impacted by a lack of stability in their family life. They want their children to have what they didn't have. They are living the biblical vision. And they are very conservative—more conservative than the theologians who led the conservative resurgence in our denomination."

That would be very conservative indeed. The conservatives who led the Southern Baptist resurgence—or what might be called the Purge—had watched with horror as their seminaries, including Southern, were overtaken by liberal sentiment. The Southern Baptist Convention became known as the "Squishy Baptist Convention." Finally they said, Enough! They would take back their church, and their cry was "Inerrancy."

Inerrancy means different things to different people. Bill Leonard, a moderate and highly respected church historian, notes at least seven schools of inerrancy, some of which hold the text itself as being inerrant, while others grant that designation to the "faith message" the text conveys. The rebelling forces were sticking close to the text. A former SBC president named Jerry Vines illustrated the position: "I'll tell you what I believe. If these fellows with their television cameras had been on that mountain that day they would have seen Jesus leave from a literal mountain, on a literal cloud, through a literal sky, in a literal body, going back to a literal heaven, to sit down on a literal throne. And in a literal body He's coming again. Literally. I really believe it."

Vines's view had, in earlier days, been without controversy and allowed no dissent. In 1879 Professor Crawford H. Toy was banished to Harvard after saying that the Great Flood "was borrowed from the Assyrians or Babylonians during or shortly before the exile." He joined the Unitarian Church—which, to be sure, was not then the church it is today. (It is Mohler who has described Unitarians as secularists with a steeple.) In 1926 the convention passed an anti-evolutionary resolution to which employees were required to pledge loyalty.

Those certainties could not hold, however, and by the late 1960s they were less likely to elicit an "amen" than an "I bet." Dr. Richard Land, now head of the SBC's Ethics and Religious Liberty Commission and a seminary student during this era, recalled that "the daily topic of discussion was about what would happen if the constituency ever found out what was being taught in our seminaries." One Southern student complained that he "was shocked in class when a professor clearly communicated that he did not believe the John 11 account that Lazarus was really dead, but that he had only fainted. He went on to explain that he doubted other biblical miracles and said, 'They must be understood in light of the existential and spiritual message of truth to the individual, whether or not the actual events are true.'"

Nancy Ammerman, a widely respected church historian, believes the SBC's seminaries were divided in half along theological lines. Conservatives, she wrote in *Baptist Battles* (1990), were especially wary of developments at Southern, Southeastern, and Midwestern, which "had almost no one willing to identify themselves as fundamentalist, and only 16 percent agreed with fundamentalist beliefs. Over half (52 percent) of their graduates were to the left of center, and over one-third (34 percent) identified themselves as moderates (eight times the proportion found in any other group of clergy)." Ammerman agrees that some professors "routinely delivered lectures designed to be 'fundamentalist busters.'" These lectures had consequences. The longer a student stayed in seminary, a survey found, the less likely he was to believe in basic Christian teachings. On the issue of the Virgin Birth, for example, 96 percent of diploma students believed fully in the event, but that number dropped to 55 percent among the master of divinity students and fell to the low thirties among the masters and doctors of theology.

Theology wasn't the only problem the conservatives set out to correct. The convention's executive leadership refused to promote the pro-life and school prayer positions popular among the rank and file. Yet it did send money to the liberal Baptist Joint Committee on Public Affairs. So far as the conservatives were concerned, the denomination had been hijacked. And so in 1978 a Texas judge named Paul Pressler, a biblical scholar named Paige Patterson, and Bill Powell, a Baptist journalist, launched the counterattack.

Patterson and Pressler went about the countryside rallying the conservative faithful and found much support for their solution to the SBC problem: elect a conservative SBC president, who in turn could name conservative trustees, who in turn could change the personnel in the executive committees and at the seminaries. In political nomenclature, they were enacting a mantra popular with another counterrevolution, this one led by Ronald Reagan: "Personnel is policy." The fruits of rebellion were soon harvested. The conservatives elected Memphis pastor Adrian Rogers to the presidency in 1979.

For liberals, this was a very troubling sign.

Adrian Rogers, like Ronald Reagan, had a highly developed talent for alienating liberals and activating conservatives. "This is going to sound almost like megalomania," he once said, "but I believe that the hope of the world lies in the West. I believe the hope of the West lies in America. I believe the hope of America is in Judeo-Christian ethics. I believe that the backbone of that Judeo-

Christian ethic is evangelical Christianity. I believe that the bell-wether of evangelical Christianity is the Southern Baptist Convention. So I believe, in a sense, that as the Southern Baptist Convention goes, so goes the world."

There was more where that came from, as Ammerman also reminds us. Bailey Smith, a popular evangelist, targeted those who rejected inerrancy: "Folks, I don't like anything that puts a question mark over the Word of God. Do you know why? Because watered-down penicillin never cured anybody." (He also stated in 1980, to widespread anguish, that "God doesn't hear the prayers of Jews.") Dallas conservative W. A. Criswell thundered that "we have not only lost our nation to the liberal, the secularist, and the humanist, but in great areas of our Baptist life we have lost our . . . institutions, our colleges, our universities. All of the Christian schools called Baptist have been lost, all of them. Brown University, McMasters University, Chicago University, there's not one that remains. And because of the inroads of liberalism and secularism the Baptist witness in the north is very small. . . . The mainline denominations of our nation have lost millions and millions these last few years. . . . It is very apparent why the decline. The curse of liberalism has sapped the strength of their message and their witness to the Lord Jesus Christ. And they point their fingers and say, 'You funny-dam-mentalists are the reason.'"

These cries from the heart, and bile duct, upset liberals—and acted as pure adrenaline to the conservatives, who began winning every presidential election. By the end of the 1988–89 academic year, one-third of Southeastern Seminary's faculty had been replaced. One by one, the other seminaries were retooled, as were the various convention agencies, including the denomination's huge publishing arm, formerly known as the Sunday School Board and now called Lifeway Christian Resources (LCR). By the mid-1990s the decidedly conservative LCR was circulating 9 million units of Sunday School curriculum each quarter from its one-million-square-foot Nashville warehouse, employing 3,000 contributing writers for magazines such as *Home Life* (circulation 500,000), *Mature Living* (345,000), *Journey* (a devotional guide for women; 145,000), *Christian Single* (65,000), *Parent Life* (115,000), and *Stand Firm*, a devotional guide for men, with 55,000 circulation. There was no theological pabulum allowed.

The convention also went on the attack politically. It found a regular target in President Bill Clinton, nominally a Southern Baptist but one who had committed various apostasies and sins, many of which were well publicized. Topping off the list of offenses, Clinton attended a liberal Methodist church in Washington with his wife, Hillary, whose cultural and social passions he often shared. In June 1996, the SBC's current president and ten previous presidents sent an open letter asking Clinton "to repent of your veto" of the Partial-Birth Abortion Ban Act. They also wanted him to enter a public forum, perhaps a prayer breakfast, and "express publicly your personal regret at having made such a decision in the first place." Clinton declined the offer.

Meanwhile, some Baptists even dragged Charles Darwin out for a drubbing. "Darwinism is the cosmic myth of the modern age," Albert Mohler told me in the mid-1990s. "Any Southern Baptist is going to reject evolution as a worldview. Scripture clearly affirms the special creation of human beings. Humans were not derivatives from prehumans." He accused liberal theologians of taking mainline churches on a "march to the sea" and attempting to hijack Scripture itself. The Jesus Seminar, he said, "tells us virtually nothing about Jesus, but a great deal about the liberal scholars who sit around with colored beads, creating a Jesus in their own image. The Jesus invented by the Jesus Seminar is a Palestinian smart aleck who sounds like a cynical and sarcastic intellectual. Coincidence?" He had harsh words for some conservatives as well,

especially neoconservatives, whose leftist origins and secular outlook had created a deep wariness in his traditionalist mind. "I am a
paleocon. I am not a neocon." Neocons are not to be trusted, he
explained, because they place "far too much hope in the political
process. How can they expect the political process to be healthier
than the culture?"

Mohler had already developed a deep pessimism about American society and where it might be heading. "A culture that casually
accepts the murder of its newborn children is probably past the
point of moral return. Be afraid. Be very afraid." Nor did he believe that the changes to the Southern Baptist Convention were ir-
reversible. "Pragmatism and postmodernism both stalk Southern
Baptists, and the gains of the last two decades can be wiped away in
less than a generation."

The years between that interview and my return visit had not
mellowed Mohler. I asked if he was not at least somewhat buoyed
by the fact that the convention and other conservative branches of
Christianity were taking on members while the mainline continued to shrink. Most administrators would be ecstatic if their organization was growing at a rate of 8 percent a year, as is the case
at Southern. Yes, he replied, he was happy about that, but this did
not distract him from the larger picture: like Father John Mc-
Closkey, he insisted that the aggregate number of self-identified
believers is misleading.

While 90 percent or so of Americans claim some relationship
to Christianity, "the number of people actually living Christian
lives is pretty low," Mohler said. "Only one in ten Americans are
regularly in church or involved in church. So I don't think the
number of committed Christians could be any higher than that."
Secularism, meanwhile, is an irresistible force. "Secularism cannot
sit still until every vestige of theism is removed from public life.
Our cultural elite is highly motivated and completely secularized

and will use its influence to push a secular agenda. And when I say secularized, I mean not accidentally secular, but positively, powerfully, and self-consciously secular."

Mohler's suggestion that only 10 percent of Christians are deeply committed to their faith was an exact echo of Father McCloskey's viewpoint regarding Catholics. I wondered if Mohler had a similarly grim view of the future.

The future, he responded, is already here—and it has much in common with some of the darker periods of the past.

"When you listen to the arguments for what is called assisted suicide, which is euthanasia, and abortion, including forms that are indistinguishable from infanticide, you hear the same logic used by the Nazis and Communists. When you hear [Princeton] Professor Paul Singer arguing that parents should be able to kill their infants, and you listen to arguments about the supposed 'duty to die,' you are hearing Nazi arguments. If humans are not seen as having been made in God's image, and thus due unconditional respect and dignity, the duty to die will sweep in. Millions can be eliminated, including the growing number of people eighty-five or older, who are going to consume a massive amount of our GDP in health care."

Talking to Albert Mohler is a mixed experience. It gives an insight into how some evangelical thinkers see the world. They are not triumphalist—quite the opposite. They are not chauvinistic, for they have little hope of stopping, on a societal scale at least, what they believe is an irresistible liberal juggernaut. Nor does this type of orthodox Christian buy into the argument that America is a shining city on the hill, or for that matter worthy of God's benevolence.

I ended our conversation by asking Mohler what he thought Jesus's view of contemporary Christianity and America might be. "Jesus knew beforehand all that was, and all that would be," he calmly replied. "There are no surprises. He spoke, in Revelation, about the church leaders who are lukewarm in their faith. They are warm spit, which he would spit out of his mouth. That is the appropriate word of judgment for much of the Christian church in America today. I find it unspeakably frightening to consider what liberal theologians will face for what they have done." As for the nation as a whole, the news was not much better. "I have every reason to assume that God would bring catastrophe on people who reject Him and His Law and actually celebrate their unbelief. God's purposes will be consummated, and one day all will be revealed."

Dr. Mohler wished me a pleasant farewell and went back to his writing, broadcasting, teaching, and perhaps brooding. I knew my interview with a second Southern Baptist leader would be entirely different, just as the grim viewpoint of Father McCloskey is offset by the more hopeful attitude of Father Richard John Neuhaus. While Albert Mohler plays the dark prophet, Dr. Richard Land is the Baptist version of the Happy Warrior. The divergence of views is a clear reminder that, despite what you hear, conservative Baptists do not all think alike.

Richard Land is head of the SBC's Ethics and Religious Liberty Commission (founded in 1913 as the Temperance and Social Service Commission), which is at the denomination's sprawling headquarters in downtown Nashville (known as the Baptist Vatican). He operates from the same religious foundation as Albert Mohler, though, as he readily agrees, his outlook is vastly more optimistic. "That could have to do with age," said Land. "I was an adult in 1968, when America was burning. Al Mohler was still a child. I know how bad it has been. I think things are much better now."

Richard Land is also a highly practiced polemicist, with a radio show, regular opinion columns, and books keeping his edge sharply honed. I had interviewed him on several previous occasions, sometimes marveling at his ability to crack a joke and slice a throat (metaphorically speaking, of course) in the same breath. He too is far out of kilter with the Baptist stereotype. Land grew up in Texas and is the product of a mixed marriage, as he puts it. His Texas roots go back six generations on his father's side, while his mother hailed from Boston—though she was a Boston Republican, which may be a primary source of his mental toughness.

He attended Princeton and went from there to Oxford University—as did Bill Clinton. He and Clinton have several other things in common besides an Ivy League education, he added: both were born in 1946, both are left-handed, both have southern accents, both have wives with doctorates—though, Land said with a smile, he is the only one of the two to honor his marriage vows, "for which my wife has expressed undying gratitude." He warmly observed that Hillary Clinton "chills a room" upon entry, though he did not suggest that as an excuse for her husband's infidelity.

Land also shares with Clinton a deep interest in politics and public affairs, and he has appeared many times before Congress as a witness for positions important to the SBC membership. He is clearly animated by a good scrap. Unlike some conservatives, he has not made it his habit to seek the approval of liberal titans or institutions, as was made clear in a 1996 denunciation of America's newspaper of record:

The New York Times *has pronounced that public policy advocacy by conservative Christians constitutes "a far greater threat to democracy than was presented by communism." Well, at least we got their attention. In many ways, people who come from the world view presented by the editorial page of the* New York

Times look upon us as alien beings. We might as well be from another planet, not just west of the Hudson. We need to understand that when we challenge their secular, relativist hegemony over American society they will react with outrage and incredulity. We must be prepared to answer their withering criticism and call it what it is—anti-religious bigotry that seeks to censor us and keep us from being involved in the public square.

If Richard Land also sounds like a preacher, it is because he is one: he preaches forty or so Sundays a year and teaches at various Southern Baptist seminaries, including Southern. When I caught up with him, he had just returned from his sixth trip to the Holy Land. I had remembered his hair as thin and graying, though now he appeared to have undergone a transformation: his hair was as thick and dark as a teenager's. His earlier views, however, were intact, and his tongue was as sharp as ever. We met for breakfast in the Southern cafeteria; we were scheduled to talk an hour, though we talked for nearly three.

Land had met with Yasir Arafat and several of his lieutenants a few days before, he said, and he had strongly denounced a recent Palestinian barbarity, which resulted in a rhetorical scuffle of sorts. The day he flew out, the founder of Hamas had taken a direct hit from an Israeli air-to-ground missile, leaving only his head intact. Nonetheless, Land was hopeful for a political solution in the Middle East. He did not, however, have a similar optimism about the future of the Protestant mainline.

"It's dead," he said, with finality.

Land has watched its decline for decades. Indeed, his first sermon, delivered in Houston when he was sixteen, was on that very topic. His text was an article in *Redbook* magazine about the theological positions held by ministers from denominations represented by the National Council of Churches. These ministers didn't believe in much, Land told his audience, including the physical resurrection of Jesus. They had cut themselves off from biblical truth and in so doing had sentenced themselves to drift and doom.

"Death was in the pot," Land said as he buttered a biscuit. "You see, once you embrace liberal Christianity, you cut loose from your anchor. And you keep drifting. Liberal Christianity had totally abandoned biblical authority by the late 1950s. They said they had 'moved beyond' Scripture." Now, he said, they have drifted over the falls, and they won't be coming back.

I asked if he thought there is only one way—his way—to read the Bible. True Christians, he responded, place themselves "under Scripture." That allows "different interpretations. That's why we have different denominations. But you cannot differ on *what* it is," he continued. "When you do that, you are standing in judgment of Scripture." Those who do so, he continued, will judge some parts wanting and ignore them. "We are not free to pick and choose what parts of Scripture to believe. I call that Dalmatian Christianity. You believe Scripture is true in spots, and those spots happen to be the things you happen to believe in." This type of Christian, he said, not only is adrift but "has no inoculation against cultural changes."

Land may share Albert Mohler's theology, but that does not lead him to the same conclusions about contemporary America. I mentioned Mohler's view that conservative Christians are under attack from nearly all directions. They live in a world where abortion on demand is allowed while prayer at high school football games is not. Their children are under constant bombardment by a highly sexual, violent, and invasive popular culture. They are watching as gay marriage draws close to legal reality and heterosexual divorce rates remain high. Parents who oppose sending their sons on camping trips with openly homosexual scout leaders are said to suffer from a psychiatric disorder. Human cloning appears to be just around the corner. "Things aren't looking so rosy in red-state America," I said.

"Really?" Land replied, eyebrows jerking upward. "I don't agree." Take the news media, he began. It had further eroded its already slender credibility by giving San Francisco Mayor Mark Newsome a free pass, if not overt praise, for encouraging gay marriage, which is illegal under California state law, while, a few months earlier, it had subjected Alabama Supreme Court judge Roy Moore to withering scorn for displaying the Ten Commandments on public property and resisting a court order to remove them. "I believe Judge Moore had the right to display the Commandments," Land said, "but I also said that he did not have the right to pick and choose which laws he would obey." But the media had shown its hand by supporting the California lawbreaker, and because the media is, for the most part, a secular bullhorn, this further diminishing of credibility was all for the better.

Perhaps so, but what about these other issues, such as gay marriage?

Land expressed little doubt, bordering on no doubt, that same-sex marriage will eventually be defeated by a constitutional amendment—after the issue wreaks havoc among liberal politicians, he added. Land, who can quote poll numbers as easily as he can Scripture, noted a Pew Trust poll indicating that 40 percent of Americans would change the way they vote solely on the basis of where the candidates stand on same-sex marriage, with 34 percent saying they would not support a candidate who supports redefinition. The animosity toward same-sex unions crosses political lines, he said, and color lines as well. He knew black ministers had told black politicians that "if you mess with marriage, I am going to bring you down," all of which, Land said, "is not good news for liberals."

Liberals, he continued, are seeking a "basic redefinition" of marriage that is doomed to failure. "It's like thinking that if you call a cat a bird it can fly." Most Americans, he said, "instinctively get this," including the "squishy middle, most of which has squished to our side." This political realignment will be aided, he said, by reminding Americans that same-sex marriage will further "imperil" Social Security.

I asked Land what he thought of homosexuality. Is it a genetic predisposition? Is there choice involved?

"Gay science," he quickly replied, "is an oxymoron. People are not born into it." More to the point, humans can choose who they have sex with and can successfully depart from homosexuality. Land knows this because the Bible says so. He quotes Paul's First Letter to the Corinthians, chapter six, in which Paul indicates that some of those in the audience he was addressing had been homosexual but were taken out of that state by the Grace of God. He added that the public might sometimes forget that the number of exclusively homosexual Americans is quite small—around 2.8 percent of men and 1.4 percent of females. Besides that, he added, it is the rare male homosexual who even wants marriage.

Land shares a politician's habit of counting noses, and on almost every issue of importance to conservative believers, he said, his side has more noses, and those numbers are increasing. The political alliance between evangelical Christians and Catholics, he said, has much improved since the time Charles Colson and Richard John Neuhaus released a statement called "Evangelicals and Catholics Together," which raised many an evangelical hackle. Indeed, a few years ago Land had told me that there were "still significant numbers of Southern Baptists who find it difficult to conceive that a person can be Roman Catholic and still a Christian." He believed that "Roman Catholicism is an errant form of Christianity. It is certainly realistic, however, that there are Roman Catholics who are fellow Christians."

These days he sings a different tune. There is much greater understanding between the two branches of the faith, he said. Evangelicals are increasingly willing to tolerate and even celebrate the worldview of conservative Catholics, he explained, as exemplified by the embrace of Mel Gibson's *The Passion of the Christ*. Central to this growing affection is that the two groups have made common cause against abortion. Now, said Land, evangelicals "are endorsing Mel, who is a pre–Vatican II Catholic. We know the Catholics better, and they know us better. I have more in common with Pope John Paul II than I do with Jimmy Carter."

This alliance, he believes, represents the "liberals' worst nightmare," and one day, he insisted, it will be strong enough to topple the core doctrine of contemporary liberalism: *Roe v. Wade*.

I must not have looked very convinced. My view is that *Roe* is going nowhere and is invoked, by both sides in the dispute, as a fund-raising and organizing tool.

Land shook his head. "We are winning the abortion issue," he insisted, noting that 2002 polling indicated a majority of Americans now believe *Roe v. Wade* was a bad decision. "The most pro-life group is eighteen- to thirty-one-year-olds. They know that one-third of their generational cohort was killed by abortion. They know that they could have been. Lots of them take that personally." Pro-life families have their babies, pro-choicers don't, he added, and parents really do have an effect on how their children think about this issue. "My professors at Princeton would be astounded to see how pro-life a modern college campus is. We have won the struggle for hearts and minds. It took the abolitionists sixty years to win. We are the abolitionists of the twentieth and twenty-first centuries. We won't stop until we have won, and if I live out a normal life span, which I intend to do, I will see victory."

That, I responded, seemed to be a very rosy scenario. It was also completely opposite to Albert Mohler's worldview, which was informed by a similar, if not identical, theology. And, one would have to add, Land's view was triumphalist to the core.

From Land's perspective, however, this is all about cold, hard facts. As I rose to leave he said there was one other number he wanted to share. "In 1960, 45 percent of registered voters were mainliners, 22 percent evangelicals, and 23 percent Roman Catholics. In 2000, 22 percent were mainliners, 31 percent evangelicals, and 33 percent Catholics. When liberals ask me why we're doing so well, I say two things. One, there are more of us than there are of you. And you ticked us off."

Richard Land smiled broadly.

"I would rather be playing our hand than theirs."

Seven

Evangelicals

Satan Had a Plan

We have mentioned, somewhat irreverently, the Wee Deity of progressive Christianity, the 30 percent God—WD-30, as it were—who makes few demands and has a decidedly small following. This is the distant deity, Jehovah's pale shadow, who lives in churches where the annual art show is taken far more seriously than the ancient injunctions of an ancient God.

The God of the Southern Baptists, the Orthodox, traditionalist Catholics, and other orthodox Christians we have met is a different matter. He has defeated death and robbed the grave of its victory. He has promised unimaginable glory to those who keep His commandments. Churches that bow in His direction are, in economic terms, experiencing the dynamic growth associated with the marketing of a superior product.

But this is not an easy God. He makes demands. He keeps tabs. And when disaster strikes, even the orthodox believer finds himself questioning His goodness, if not His very existence. If God is indeed omniscient and omnipresent, why does He allow disaster to occur, especially to those who have so closely cast their lot with Him?

These are serious questions for serious believers—and for those who represent the orthodox God from the pulpit and face these questions on a regular basis. Ministers, especially those at smaller churches, may read nearly as much Scripture at graveside as from the pulpit, sometimes under conditions that test even their faith.

Some funerals are harder than others. And for an outsider, some funerals raise a set of questions more difficult still: How, for instance, does an orthodox Christian minister preach the omnipotent loving God to a mother whose son has just been shot dead while eating lunch in the school library? How does he go on believing in such a God, year after year? Would it not be much easier, and perhaps reasonable, to believe in a God who plays no direct role in human affairs, who had not seen all horror before it occurred and allowed it to proceed nonetheless?

I knew a man who could answer these questions with more authority than most. He is the Rev. Bill Oudemolen. He has conducted some of the hardest funerals one can imagine, including a service that broadcast the orthodox response to wrenching horror to a stunned world—a large portion of which, we can reasonably assume, could hardly believe what it was hearing.

Bill Oudemolen and Brian Boone were out for a drive on April 20, 1999, enjoying the view of the Colorado Rockies from Route C-470, which runs along the front range outside Denver. Oudemolen and Boone, his associate pastor, were taking a short break from their duties at Foothills Bible Church, an evangelical mainstay in the suburban community of Littleton, hard by near the foothills. This was a glorious glimpse of spring, one of the first warm days of the year. A minister like himself might have been put in mind of rebirth on such a day, that spring always follows winter just as Easter follows Good Friday.

Suddenly, a dozen or so emergency vehicles raced past. Something big is up, Oudemolen said. There was no question: they had to follow. Who knows, perhaps their services might be needed.

Oudemolen and Boone soon found themselves at the corner of Pierce and Bowles Avenues, which form the east and north boundaries of Clement Park. "It was total chaos," Oudemolen recalled. "Children were running around screaming. I rolled the window down and asked one of them what was going on. She cried out, 'Someone's in the school shooting people.'" Oudemolen parked across the street. He and Boone ran back to the park, which was filling with students. "Some kids were screaming. Some were laughing or giggling. Some were lying on the ground moaning. Some were saying they had seen dead bodies."

At about this time, I was putting on a CD at my local gym in Virginia. I looked up at the bank of televisions in front of the treadmills. The Fox News Channel had its NEWS ALERT logo posted. Nothing new there. If a roofer in Omaha hits his thumb with a hammer, it seems to rate a NEWS ALERT. But there was something captivating about the picture on the screen. Children were running out of a building that looked familiar, though the full connection wasn't made until the name flashed across the bottom of the screen: Columbine High School—Littleton, Colorado.

Columbine had been our neighborhood school. The park that was filling with students, where Bill Oudemolen and Brian Boone were just beginning to confront hell on earth, was the park where my two sons played football and practiced lacrosse during our six years in Colorado. Witnesses were saying they had heard shooting and explosions inside the school. I began thinking of the children from our old neighborhood who would probably be there today—Bobby, Kevin, Dusty, and most of the kids from the teams, and all those beautiful young girls from my oldest son's class. I headed for home, where I assumed he would already have arrived.

Oudemolen immediately took out his cell phone and told students to call their parents and tell them they had made it to safety. Massive numbers of police were now arriving. "They were all crouched down in that formation that everyone has now seen a thousand times. I just couldn't figure out why they weren't going into the school." A helicopter flew over and everyone hit the ground, he added, but it was only a news chopper. The media were also arriving in force. Students prayed, laughed, and cried, and some now gave interviews. Yes, they had heard shots. One student pointed out that this was Hitler's birthday and that the date may have had some significance. There was talk of students in black trench coats. One student had heard someone scream, "This is a good day to die." A teacher from Oudemolen's congregation ran to him screaming, "I'll never get over this." They prayed. "Lord, we need you. We don't know what is going on, but something dark is going on."

When I got home, my oldest son was watching the coverage. He would have been a senior, and since he rarely missed school he would likely have been there today. We saw familiar faces on the screen, including the sister of a former girlfriend. She had not been able to find her sister, she said. We also wondered if his best friend Bobby had gotten out. At this point, there was no talk of how many people might have been hurt. But enough police were there now to take on an armored division, still cowering outside. "What in the hell are they waiting for?" my son said. All I could think to say was, "Must be waiting for the doughnut truck."

Oudemolen continued passing around his phone, occasionally commandeering it to touch base with his staff. It was quickly agreed that the church would open that evening for prayers and hold a prayer service the next morning. He asked if anything had been heard from congregation families with children at Columbine. Oudemolen also learned that parents looking for their children were being asked to go either to the small public library on the west side of the park or to Leawood Elementary School, a few blocks from Columbine. Perhaps he should see if his services were needed there.

As Oudemolen entered the library, a distraught woman begged him to talk with her daughter. She was crying that she had hidden in a cabinet in the library and when she came out had seen many dead schoolmates scattered around the room. The mother insisted that she was simply frightened and confused. "The girl fell into my arms," said Oudemolen. "She was screaming that she had seen bodies. She screamed at her mother, 'I saw dead bodies!'"

By now, a Columbine father had called 911 to say that he feared his son might be involved in the shootings. The son's name was Eric Harris.

Oudemolen continued providing what comfort he could but increasingly felt "a strong need to be with my wife." He broke free and drove home, where his wife Nan had put together a list of families with Columbine students. They began making their fearful rounds.

It was quick work, he said. They'd drive up the driveway, Nan would exit and knock on the door, and the parents would quickly open up and report that their son or daughter had been accounted for. At one stop, however, there was disturbing news. John Tomlin was still missing. Nan was told that his parents were already over at Leawood Elementary.

The gym at Leawood had been organized to reunite students with their parents in as orderly a fashion as possible. When a busload of students arrived, Oudemolen said, they would be brought inside and directed onto a small stage. Their names would be announced. Parents and children would scream as they were reunited; massive joy erupting alongside the unfathomable anxiety of families whose children were still missing. The platform would slowly empty, and then the next busload would arrive.

Doreen and John Tomlin were still waiting when the Oudemolens arrived. So were several other parents, some with children. Each family was surrounded by a small group of people, often including a pastor, Oudemolen recalled. "The women in the small groups were usually sitting in chairs, and the men were standing around them."

By seven, there were no more arrivals.

Six or seven families and their supporters were still waiting. "There would be periods of calm," Oudemolen said, "then a sudden wave of emotion and panic. We would all just bow our heads and pray. We'd say, 'Lord, we need your strength. We can't do this on our own.' We stayed until about nine-thirty. A sheriff's deputy started making the rounds. He arrived at our group and said he didn't think there would be any more announcements tonight. He also said they did know there had been fatalities. Specifically, he said, there had been a significant amount of killing in the library."

Doreen Tomlin was stricken: "John always had lunch in the library on Tuesdays."

The police report on the Columbine massacre says that the first students shot were Rachel Scott and Richard Castaldo. They were among the students "taking advantage of the spring day by eating their lunches outside, relaxing on the grassy areas around the school building." Photographs show that Rachel Scott was a beautiful girl, and like many young people in this community, she was a vibrant Christian. In her backpack was her diary, whose most current entry read:

> *When will the world open and see*
> *The art in me*
> *I write not for the sake of glory, not for the sake of fame, not for the*
> *   sake of success*
> *But for the sake of my soul*
> *Days of routine are killing me*
> *I won't be labeled as average*

Rachel Scott was the first to die. When investigators opened her backpack, they found her journal. It had also been pierced by a bullet—which cut a hole just after the last word of this final entry.

The report does not say if she was shot by Eric Harris or his colleague, Dylan Klebold. Klebold was later identified as the "follower" who was somehow led astray by Harris, who is said to have accorded most people the same status he did insects.

Klebold was remembered as a seemingly normal child who pitched baseball for youth teams. As he grew older, a neighborhood mother recalled, he would sometimes become upset when games didn't go his way. But he did not reveal a threatening manner. She welcomed him into her home, as she also welcomed my younger son, who saw Klebold there on occasion. Whatever interaction they had would later take on a morbid nature; the hand that may have opened the door in front of my son or tossed him a ball was the hand that held the gun that killed John Tomlin.

The last moments of John Tomlin's life in the Columbine library are well documented. According to the police report, Eric Harris walked to one table "where he bent down and saw two frightened girls. He slapped the table top twice, said, Peek-a-boo, and fired, killing Cassie Bernall." Harris may have been struck in the face by the recoiling gun. He then turned on Bree Pasquale, who was sitting nearby on the floor, and asked her if she wanted to die (she was unable to get beneath a nearby table because there was no room left). She began to plead for her life. Harris seemed disoriented, the report said, and may have been bleeding from the nose or mouth. He did not shoot Bree Pasquale. The reason may have been that Dylan Klebold called his attention to another table under which two boys were hiding. One of the boys, Klebold shouted, was black. This was Isaiah Shoels. At this point, the report says, Harris was heard to start laughing and say, "Everyone's gonna die. We're gonna blow up the school anyway."

Klebold made a racial comment, the report continues, then "began grabbing at Isaiah Shoels in an effort to pull him out from underneath the table. Harris fired under the table, killing Isaiah. Klebold fired under the table as well, killing Matthew Kechter."

Klebold walked around a bit, then shot and wounded Mark Kintgen. He then shot under a nearby table, wounding both Valeen Schnurr and Lisa Kreutz. Walking beside the table, Klebold proceeded to fire as fast as his gun would shoot, killing Lauren Townsend. Harris, meantime, looked under another table where two girls hid. He was heard to say, "Pathetic," but did not shoot. Valeen Schnurr, critically wounded, began to cry, "Oh God, help me." Klebold was heard to taunt her about her belief in God, but then walked away.

John Tomlin's time had come. He was hiding under what came to be known as "Table 6" with a student named Nicole Nowlen. Harris fired under the table, wounding both. "Tomlin came out from under the table and Klebold shot and killed him," the report says. A camera in the library showed that the gunmen had apparently become dejected, perhaps because propane-tank bombs they had placed in the cafeteria didn't explode, even though they shot directly into the tanks after their detonators had failed. By some estimates, these bombs would have killed several hundred students.

Surrounded by pools of blood and the dead and wounded, Harris and Klebold convened the final act. A witness heard one or perhaps both count, "One, two, three," then heard shots fired. It was over: a dozen students and one teacher dead, along with Harris and Klebold. John Tomlin was sixteen.

His parents were not sure he was dead until the next day. Oudemolen had just concluded the 1:00 P.M. prayer service when he got a call from a staffer who had been with the Tomlins. The police had just come and confirmed John's death. Oudemolen drove to the Tomlin house to make plans for the funeral.

———

I met Bill Oudemolen in the early 1990s at another funeral, this one for a friend who had died young of breast cancer, leaving behind a husband and three young sons. I was struck that afternoon by two things: Oudemolen's dramatic pompadour and a statement he made during the funeral. Standing dark-suited in his pulpit, looking down at the children and the widower, he stated forcefully that not only was their mother in a much better place than she had ever been, but even if it were possible for her to return to them she would not do so.

I had had little experience with evangelical Christianity at the time, and Oudemolen was evangelical to the core. Raised in the Reformed Church, he got his theological training at Grand Rapids Baptist Bible College, which is every bit as progressive, he later cracked, as it sounds. I was so stunned by his statement to the family, which he followed with an altar call, that I wrote a newspaper column in which I quoted the line. This led to a subsequent call and a discussion in which Oudemolen simply said that he believed every word of what he said.

Death is where "the rubber meets the road" regarding religious faith, he said. He had good news to share, and there are few better places to share it than a funeral. His job, after all, is to save souls, whenever and wherever possible. At funerals, people's minds are on eternal matters. This is how an evangelical pastor buries the dead—and saves the living. That was his explanation, made without apology.

I had lost track of Oudemolen until the time of the massacre. But it seemed likely he would do at least one of the Columbine funerals. Littleton is home to several large evangelical churches. His Foothills Bible Church is within a half-mile of two other evangelical churches of similar size (3,500 or so members). As it turned out, John Tomlin's was the first of the Columbine funerals. This guaranteed international media coverage, including a pool camera inside the church. The whole world would hear what an evangelical pastor had to say about this unspeakable event.

There was no shortage of commentary, incrimination, invective, and speculation from elsewhere. Violent video games and music were blamed for inspiring the mass murder. Suburban indifference was also said to have played a role. And if this could happen in Littleton, which is solidly middle- and upper-middle-class—the killers drove to the killings in a booby-trapped BMW—it could most definitely happen anywhere. There was great apprehension that Columbine would touch off a streak of copycat mass murders.

Against this fevered backdrop, Oudemolen took to his pulpit. He had never addressed the world before. He knew he would be speaking not only to a stunned world, but to one that would probably be stunned by the message he planned to deliver. But he was sticking to it. His task was to make sense of all this—while maintaining that the universe is ruled by a loving God. Only one explanation would suffice. Satan.

Oudemolen quickly got to his point (these passages are slightly edited):

On Tuesday morning at Columbine High School the forces of evil converged to unleash a violent and bloody spring holocaust on teens and their teachers. Two suicides followed thirteen homicides. A morning of mayhem led to a horrific afternoon and evening of waiting. We have parents sitting here today who were part of that waiting. Riveting reunions between parents and kids brought tearful relief to hundreds throughout that dark day. Sadly, some parents left Leawood Elementary School without a reunion. Many reunions took place in hospitals and funeral

homes across our community. John and Doreen Tomlin were one
of the first couples to see their son in a funeral home.

The Tomlins sat in the front row, just on the other side of their
son's coffin from the pulpit. Oudemolen often looked over to them
as he spoke.

On April 20, 1999, Satan had a plan for Littleton. We know it
was Satan who had a grip on those two boys because he left his
calling cards—death, destruction, and dread. Make no mistake:
Tuesday's atrocity is not simply about black trench coats, pur-
ported parental failure, anemic gun laws, inattentive teachers,
or Marilyn Manson. Ultimately, what we saw on Tuesday came
from Satan's home office—the pit of hell. In fact, I believe I
smelled hell. On Tuesday I believe I got as close as you can get on
earth to smelling hell—right there at the corner of Pierce and
Bowles.

Oudemolen, it is worth remembering, does not consider Satan
a mere symbol of evil. He is a real being, and for all Oudemolen
knew, Satan was lurking nearby as he spoke.

Satan had a plan for Littleton, and his plan was that we would
be overcome by fear, hatred, and, finally, inconsolable grief. In-
consolable grief can ruin your life. That's not to say there's not a
place for grieving. Five days after this episode, we are all still
shocked and grieving.
Satan had a plan on Tuesday, but I don't think it worked.
Why? Because God also had a plan.
Proverbs 19:21 says, "Many are the plans in a man's heart,
but it is the Lord's purpose that prevails." Genesis 50, the story
of Joseph, reminds us that what Joseph's brothers intended for

evil, what they intended for harm, what they intended for hate, God intended for good. I love those words "but God."

Satan's plan for Littleton was fear, hate, and inconsolable grief. God's plan, which went into action immediately, is for power, love, and sound thinking.

As I said earlier, I don't want to appear glib or preachy today, but if we're going to turn to God in this crisis, we have to turn to God believing that God is able to do abundantly above and beyond anything we can ask or think. I want to be one voice in this community saying, "God is still in control; God is good; and God has amazing plans for us until Jesus Christ returns to this earth."

God wants people of Littleton and the world to see and experience his power. I want to tell you, God's power was evident in the middle of this bloodbath.

By now, heads were bound to be shaking around the world. A few were no doubt shaking inside Foothills Bible Church. But Oudemolen also believed that a few heads that had shaken before at the mention of Satan would now be nodding. He was planting seeds. And the time had now come for harvesting seeds planted earlier.

It was time for the altar call.

This past Wednesday night friends of John Tomlin were having a meeting. One of his friends, Brandon, had been witnessed to by John. Brandon had not yet accepted Christ as his Savior. But on Wednesday night, when the man leading the meeting said, "Would anyone like to receive Christ?" Brandon said, "I want to."

The man said, "I want you to be sure. I don't want this to be an emotional decision. I know you're all stirred up by all of this."

*Brandon said, "John has been talking to me about this. I
know exactly what the Gospel is. I'm going to receive Christ
tonight."*

*On Friday morning John and Doreen said to me, "We want
John Robert Tomlin's service to be an evangelistic service. We want
you to give an invitation to receive Christ. We know that won't
erase the pain of the loss of our son. But please present the Gospel."*

Oudemolen knew that some people, and perhaps a lot of
people, would be appalled by his making an altar call at such a
time. He had been criticized in print for this very thing. He didn't
miss a step.

*Some of you are probably thinking, "Bill, we're still grieving.
How can you be so loud and positive about what's going on? This
is a horrible tragedy."*

*I know. I think I feel it as deeply as anyone who didn't have
someone in the school can feel it. We had kids from this church in
that school. There's a mom and dad in the front row who know
exactly what I'm talking about.*

*However, what I want to say to you is God has a plan, and
his plan is to turn evil into good.*

*John and Doreen's abiding faith in the Lord has amazed
me. The father of Rachel Scott has also amazed me. I asked him,
"Do you have any anger toward the boys or their families that
have done this?"*

*He said, "I don't, and I probably should. But I feel like I'm
blanketed by a covering of God's Grace."*

*I saw the parents of Cassie Bernall in an interview, and they
amazed me also. They've been bold in saying, "We believe the
Lord can use this for his glory."*

None of us in this room would ever have chosen what hap-

pened on Tuesday to happen. That was Satan's plan. But in the midst of this horrendous tragedy, God also has a plan. God's light is bringing people to the Truth, and God's power is real. Before we leave today, I'm going to ask you if you've put your faith in him. If you haven't, then maybe you've been moved to a place where you've decided, "Today is the day for me. I need Jesus in my life."

Oudemolen asked those who were ready to come to Jesus to raise their hands, and then pressed on to his conclusion.

I don't know about you, but I will never be the same. I don't think I have any choice. We are being shaped by a tragedy that will mark us for the rest of our lives. Only time will tell whether the city of Littleton will be known for God's power, God's love, and God's clear thinking. When we choose that, we choose God's plan and God's glory over the plans of his enemy.

I talked with Bill Oudemolen just after the fifth anniversary of the massacre. He had the calm and somewhat resigned nature I remembered him having, perhaps made more so by health problems. Most of the men in his family die young, he said; their hearts give out. His heart had given him some trouble as well, and he was now into his fifties, well into the danger zone. He was self-depreciating and spoke gently. His tone was not one of jarring certitude. "This is what I believe" was his message, not, "This is what you must believe."

Had Columbine changed his life? I asked. "I think of it every day," he said. Especially when driving near the school. "I may be going to the dentist, and there it is. I don't obsess on it, but it is there." He saw little possibility that this would ever change.

How did he think his funeral message had been received? His tone brightened. He felt it had gone over very well with the most important part of his audience. "At one point during the service I looked down and made eye contact with Doreen. I would not begin to say that she looked happy, but she did look like this was helping her. She was at her own son's funeral, and God was giving peace to her." I noted that he had not used the line about the departed not coming back even were that possible. "I have had reason to think about that line since that funeral," he said, with slight amusement. "I know it sounds harsh, especially to children, but I do believe the substance of it."

How did he think his "devil talk" had gone over, especially with a worldwide audience? "I was quoted a great deal when I talked about smelling the presence of Satan," Oudemolen replied. "I too was in shock, like everyone there. But I did know that what was going on was ultimately about darkness and evil. This is core theology. Lucifer is a fallen angel, running to and fro about the earth. He is the enemy of our soul. I know this seems antiquated and old-fashioned, dusty as having a house without electricity, no car, horses and buggies. But I believe that Lucifer is as real as God. That is what my life's experience has taught me."

Did that mean he believes Satan had directed Harris and Klebold? "I don't take the human responsibility out of it. They made the pipe bombs and pulled the triggers. I'm not saying they were unwitting tools of Satan. But I do believe there was demonic and satanic involvement. These were boys, not demons, but I do believe it is possible to become possessed by demonic spirits, to act in concert with demonic activity."

Five years had passed—plenty of time to let the horror sink in and wonder, every day perhaps, why a loving God would allow such a thing to happen. Had Columbine shaken his personal faith?

"I sit in my office, or lie in bed at home falling asleep at night, and I ask, 'God what *are* you up to permitting something like this?'" Oudemolen replied softly. "I believe that God has a transcendent story that will answer these questions. I believe God does not orchestrate these events, but he does permit them. And I wonder why they are permitted. It is something I cannot grasp. I do see through a glass darkly and will not have the full picture until I am in heaven. But for now, I can't make sense of it. I can't say that as a result of Columbine here are fifteen good things that have happened, such as children coming to the Lord or the Gospel going out."

I had one more question. This had been the toughest funeral of his career—hadn't it?

Well, Oudemolen replied, maybe not. He had buried many people. During his first seven years of ministry he averaged one funeral a week. There was one a few years ago that was perhaps harder than John Tomlin's.

A member of his church, a young mother, had murdered her two children. Severe depression was blamed. "There was one child-sized casket," he said. "Inside, the three-year-old brother had his arm around his sister, who was only a couple of months old. It was an unbelievably traumatic situation." But the story did not end there, Oudemolen said. He and his wife Nan regularly visited the mother during her incarceration in a state mental facility. She was released after three years. She is back at Foothills Bible Church.

Bill Oudemolen wasn't the only preacher called on to minister to Columbine families. Other sermons took different approaches. How was the community to think about Eric Harris and Dylan Klebold? How could residents of Littleton keep a check on the anger and hatred that could so easily consume them?

In his post-Columbine sermon, Nick Lillo, pastor at Littleton's Centennial Community Church, told of visiting a massive makeshift memorial dedicated to the victims. "There was a hand-painted sign propped up against a tree at Clement Park that said, 'These flowers and prayers are for the innocent victims and their families, NOT for the two monsters that committed this selfish act,'" he began. "One lady who was there to leave a bouquet of flowers saw the sign, and when she saw that sign whispered to no one in particular, 'I want to give them to the monsters too.'"

I have been thinking long and hard and asking myself, were these kids really monsters? No question, they did monstrous things. Part of me wants to say that they were, but I wonder if I want to do that so I can say they are not like the rest of us. They are not like me. That is what we want to believe, because that is what makes it easier to make sense of our lives. But were they monsters? I do not know.

I do know this: I do know that we all have good and bad within us. Each one here has potential for incredible good and horrific evil. True, none of us would commit mass murder—that seems off the scale. But we too have the struggle within us, we too have an incredible capacity for evil in our own way. They were not always monsters. As I read about them this week, I read about kids who liked baseball, kids that were exceptionally bright, kids who had friends of other races, kids that seemed normal when they were small and young. But something went wrong. Something happened to bring about so much hate. Something turned them from normal kids to monstrous kids. These young men fed the dark side of their souls.

Like Bill Oudemolen, Nick Lillo tried to find something positive in the horror. He reminded his congregation that they live in a world of pain and that perhaps they could take something from this experience to help make this world a bit less painful:

Someone told me this week that every fifteen minutes in Kosovo fifteen people are killed. That was easy for me, and maybe for you, to block out before this, but now we know what some of that pain is like. Suddenly we are not so callous. Suddenly we have an opportunity to open our eyes and care way beyond ourselves. Perhaps after this tragedy it will no longer be so easy to turn on the evening news and hear about lives lost and simply block out of our minds and our hearts—even if it is thousands of miles away. Just maybe these events will make us more compassionate and loving. Maybe it will help us be people with bleeding hearts.

These were hard funerals. But they did offer hope. The dead had ascended, and those left behind could make something good out of the bad that had been done. Just as God had brought order out of chaos to create this world, He could bring love and purpose from hatred. One day the veil would be lifted and even this inexplicable act would make sense. Until then, they had to take whatever good they could find and soldier on.

Not all the Columbine funerals were conducted by evangelicals, nor were they all conducted for the innocent victims. Eric Harris and Dylan Klebold also had to be buried. For a minister, this would be perhaps the toughest assignment of his career. Dylan Klebold, for instance, not only had helped murder thirteen people but had hoped, along with Harris, to kill many hundreds more in the school cafeteria. There were indications that at one time the two had hoped to take hostages, commandeer a jetliner, and crash it into Manhattan.

Klebold's funeral was conducted by the Rev. Don Marxhausen, a Lutheran who had been the Klebold family pastor some six or eight years before the killings. The family had attended his church for several months, according to published accounts, but lost interest in organized religion. Their agony was compounded by reports that the massacre was apparently scheduled to coincide with Adolf Hitler's birthday. Klebold's mother is Jewish, and the family celebrated both Passover and Christmas.

Only a handful of people attended the service, according to an account in *Christian Century* magazine. Marxhausen quoted from the Old and New Testaments, including the story of King David and his son Absalom:

O, my son! Absalom, my son, my son Absalom! Would that I had died instead of you.

He also read the Twenty-third Psalm and the Lord's Prayer. Like his evangelical counterparts, Marxhausen attempted, in his brief message, to offer at least a fragment of hope:

God, who raises up and lifts up after the journey through the valley, will do so in time and in surprising ways. Some people will run from you, there will be others who will come to you. There is God's mercy, and there is the mercy of others. True enough, there will be those who do not know Grace and will want to give only judgment. But God will reach out to you through those who know His Grace. I have no idea how you are going to heal. God still wants to reach out to you and will always reach out to you in some way.

Marxhausen seems to have made the best of a very hard situation. While Oudemolen could offer hope and the promise of ultimate meaning, Marxhausen did not come from a tradition that allowed such a certain response. Nor did the family he ministered to. He could only say that God might bring the survivors comfort, though he had no idea how. It was a thin reed in a terrible wind, but all that was available.

Two families, two sons, two deaths, two responses.

Marxhausen's most noted line came just after a memorial service for the victims that was attended by seventy thousand people: "I felt like I'd been hit over the head with Jesus." Oudemolen stuck to the old text: we see through a glass darkly and must live on by faith and trust until the veil is lifted. Similarly, Nick Lillo counseled members of a deeply shaken community to remember the evil in their own hearts as they considered the evil of those who slaughtered their children.

And the Tomlins went on worshiping the orthodox God who knew, at the foundation of time, that on April 20, 1999, their son would be eating lunch in a high school library in one of the nation's most idyllic states. Suddenly he would hear gunfire and see classmates, boys and girls, torn apart. As the killers came his way he would crouch under a table, but there would be no safe harbor that day. He would soon be discovered and wounded. He would come bleeding from beneath the table and be shot dead. A dozen others would die, besides the assailants, and in the aftermath one mother would find the burden of grief too powerful to overcome and kill herself.

And still the Tomlins believe. On Sunday mornings they sit in Oudemolen's church, perhaps near a woman who murdered her two children, all pursuing Truth in the shadow of an ancient cross. These are not frivolous people. They are worthy of their God.

Eight

Evangelists

Damascus Roads

Saturday mornings in America have their own rituals: sports practices, cartoons, large breakfasts, grocery shopping, yard work, home repair, and, for some, nursing a hangover. Many Americans with experience in that last pursuit will attest that the later one stays up Friday night, the greater the chance of a knock at the door the next morning, sometime around nine-fifteen, from an evangelist.

This evangelist is never, ever a Unitarian. It will be highly unlikely that he or she is a Methodist, Presbyterian, or Episcopalian. It is much more likely that one will be greeted by a Jehovah's Witness, a Mormon, or some type of evangelical Christian. This is part of the religious duty, a demand of the faith. There is an idea among these people that God wants them out spreading the Word. They take their great commission seriously.

Evangelizing, among other things, distinguishes them from their progressive counterparts. It is one reason why their churches are filling instead of emptying. To employ a biological metaphor, evangelizing (which takes many forms) is how religions project themselves into the future. It is a form of religious procreation. Progressive churches, like many of their members, do not excel in replication. They may fancy themselves smarter, and they may be wealthier. They may die surrounded by the best appliances available. They will have lived large, but failed to pass on their religion.

Thus, they will have taken their faith further down the road to extinction.

Evangelizing takes many forms, some of which are quite unusual. Associated Press writer Mark Thiessen filed a story in December 2003 informing us that the Latter-Day Saints had angered the Russian Orthodox Church by "buying the names of dead souls" and rebaptizing them into the Mormon faith. This process is known as proxy-baptism. As Thiessen explains, "The LDS church has long collected names from government documents and other records worldwide, then made them available for use in temple rituals, during which Mormon stand-ins are immersed in water to offer the dead salvation and entry to the Mormon religion." This has resulted in some big catches, including Adolf Hitler, Anne Frank, and a few popes. Many estimable Jews have also been rebaptized, including David Ben-Gurion, Israel's first prime minister, and Theodor Herzl, the founder of Zionism. As it happens, the Rev. Sun Myung Moon has also claimed that Hitler and Joseph Stalin have responded to his postmortem evangelical initiatives and now recognize him as the Messiah. Any soul, it seems, is a terrible thing to waste.

Most of the time, however, evangelizing is the act of sharing the faith with another (live) person that requires two things: a willingness to share and the willingness to go out and find someone to share with. Such was the process by which Christianity began and prospered, and now, in progressive churches, its absence accompanies decline.

Barna Research, the California polling and marketing company cited in chapter 3, tells us that evangelizing is more of a passion among conservative believers, especially Protestants. Quoting 2004 survey information, Barna noted that "Catholics (22%) are less likely than Protestants (47%) to feel a responsibility to share their faith with others." Born-again Christians are especially active: 78 percent had shared their faith in the past year by offering to pray with a non-Christian person; 49 percent had taken a non-Christian friend to church. Demographically speaking, "49% of Blacks strongly agree that they 'personally have a responsibility to tell other people about their religious belief' versus 36% of Hispanics, 33% of whites and 33% of Asians." Southerners (41 percent) feel a greater need to share their faith than midwesterners (35 percent), westerners (also 35 percent), and those living in the Northeast (26 percent). Barna also pointed out that if you're going to bring people into the fold, it's best to get them while they're young: while children age five to thirteen have a 32 percent probability of accepting Jesus Christ as their Savior, that number drops to 4 percent at ages fourteen to eighteen and rises only slightly, to 6 percent, for those over eighteen.

Evangelizing seldom makes the papers, unless of course the convert is a dead dictator. Yet conservative Christians are always about it, sometimes gathering massive numbers of people together for this very purpose. The "Urbana '03" mission convention, for instance, held in Urbana, Illinois, on December 27–31, 2003, hosted nineteen thousand students, missionaries, and religious leaders. These were people who take the Book seriously: "Each morning," said an account posted on a religion-focused Web site, "students gathered in small-group Bible studies in their dormitories, then walked in the unusually warm weather or rode buses to the Assembly Hall, the university's basketball arena, where they heard general-session teachings based on the Gospel of Luke." About half the participants were Asian, Hispanic, black, or American Indian. By event's end, ten thousand students had committed to becoming missionaries. The sponsorship reflects the fact that this was not a mainline event: InterVarsity Christian Fellowship, the Madison, Wisconsin–based evangelical campus ministry; InterVarsity Christian Fellowship of Canada; and Groupes Bibliques

Universitaires et Collègiaux du Canada. On the last night of the convention, the heads of four other large campus Christian organizations prayed for one another onstage: Youth for Christ, Campus Crusade for Christ, Young Life, and The Navigators.

These efforts are augmented by a great deal of "self-evangelizing." A *New York Times* story published January 31, 2004, quoted an estimate by the Pew Internet and American Life Project that "by December 2002, 35 million Americans had searched for religious or spiritual information online, compared with 36 million who had downloaded music files." Calvin College professor Quentin J. Schultze has called the Internet "a deeply evangelistic medium. The influence of religious evangelists has been greatly underreported."

I know one evangelist whose story is not necessarily underreported, but who is one of the most vibrant contemporary reminders that Christianity, and especially orthodox Christianity, is still capable of transforming lives to such a stunning degree that even nonbelievers may suspect, however briefly, that a supernatural hand is at work. Paul of Tarsus was one such convert. The one I had in mind is Charles Colson. Chuck Colson's religious transformation is one of the most dramatic in modern American history, and it produced an equally dramatic result: the prison ministry he founded after he accepted Jesus is the largest in the world. Colson is a Southern Baptist for whom Jesus is the Son of God, the only hope for salvation. He does not preach progressive Christianity.

His story is well known. Colson left the public sector in the early 1970s under duress, owing to Watergate-related problems. One media appraisal during his White House years said Colson was "incapable of humanitarian thought." In 1974 he went to jail (Maxwell Prison, Alabama), where he spent seven months. He had gone from being Richard Nixon's special counsel—the second most powerful man in the world by some accounts—to waxing floors, raking leaves, and emptying the trash. He had also become a Christian shortly before his incarceration.

In 1976 Colson founded Prison Fellowship Ministries; his worldwide ministry now boasts forty thousand volunteers in one hundred countries, and his Angel Tree Ministry provides Christmas presents to half a million children of inmates each year. He has written twenty books, which have collectively sold more than five million copies. He also has a daily radio feature carried on one thousand radio outlets. He is co-author, with Richard John Neuhaus, of the book *Evangelicals and Catholics Together,* for which he lost a great deal of support among evangelicals, though, as we shall see, that tide has turned.

I wanted to talk to Colson about the decline of the mainline and the problems faced by evangelicals who hope to advance orthodox Christianity. I should point out here a prior professional arrangement. I met Colson in the mid-1990s in Colorado. As it happened, I was in the private sector, under duress, looking to move back east and start anew as a freelance writer. Colson was in the market for someone to help him write a once-a-week secular newspaper column. I took Colson on as my first client (Colson might say he took me on as a ghost). My family and I packed up, left Littleton (we would be especially thankful for this on April 20, 1999), and headed to the Washington, D.C., metropolitan region, where Prison Fellowship keeps its offices. This arrangement, like most ghostwriting jobs, lasted a few years. I was amused, sometime afterward, when Colson came under criticism for using unacknowledged writers. I have ghostwritten for many people and in fact did an entire book after interviewing the client for a full one hour and forty-five minutes. I have written newspaper columns for newspaper columnists who don't have time to do their own writing. I have written speeches for a presidential hopeful who relied on me to choose the focus issue in the speech—in effect, to develop her positions as I went along. Colson, on the other hand, went over every word and every piece of punctuation. He was by far the most hands-on client I've ever had.

That could be taxing, but there was compensation besides money—Colson has great stories, many of which came from his years at the right hand of Richard Nixon. He used some as Christian apologetics. One example stands out. Colson scoffs at the idea that the Resurrection was a conspiracy, as some scholars and authors insist. By this theory, the apostles simply decided to tell the world that Jesus had risen from the dead, perhaps as a way to advance his teachings, and also as a way to increase their own historic stature.

Yet Jesus's inner circle, Colson reasonably argues, was made up of powerless men, many of whom went to their deaths insisting that they had seen the Risen Christ. By comparison, Colson and his associates in Nixon's inner circle were among the most powerful men in the world. With the mere suggestion of possible incarceration, however, much deal-cutting ensued. (I assumed from the outset that it was not advisable to speak the name John Dean in Colson's presence.) His conclusion: Jesus's followers believed, with every fiber of their being, that Jesus had risen from the dead. People will die for what they believe is the Truth, but they will not die for something they know to be a lie.

Colson also had riveting stories about his work in prisons. He has been especially appalled by prison conditions in Central and South America, where he would find thirty to forty men jammed into a single cell with a bucket for a toilet. Some died within, others went insane, and some were converted to Christianity. Colson told one story about preaching in a Southern Hemisphere prison that included a substantial transvestite contingent. The scene he set is unforgettable: packed prison; hot, reeking air; desperate and crazed inmates and inquisitive transvestites, all hearing the Gospel preached by a Boston-born, Ivy League–educated (Brown), former Republican henchman. Colson had come a long way.

I began our conversation by asking Colson his view on the problems within old-line Protestantism.

"The mainline decline," he began, "continues because these churches are neither fish nor fowl. They are far too eager to accommodate themselves to the culture." The accommodation began in earnest in the 1960s, he said, though unlike many conservatives, he had good things to say about that contentious decade, the one that brought Richard Nixon and himself to power. "The sixties were laudable in their effort to bring social justice to society," Colson said. At the same time, this was the period when Christian orthodoxy began to seriously weaken in the mainline. Liberal churches did good things for many people. But they also became less spiritually relevant. "People want the real thing. They are not interested in a pale substitute, because it can never satisfy. It just doesn't answer the questions people have."

Today, he said, many churches that are presumed to be orthodox, at least compared with mainline churches, are making the same mistake. This is especially true in some of the large evangelical churches, which Colson said are purveyors of "self-centered worship. You may get people to come to those churches, and you may have church growth. But you will not have church impact. The reason is that church becomes increasingly like the culture. People go in, see a skit, listen to some music, hear a soothing sermon, and think they've done their Christian duty. They are entering the exact precarious position the mainline found itself in in the sixties and seventies." As such, these churches may eventually see their own pews empty. What churches should be doing, Colson said, is teaching believers that Christianity offers a sound and rational explanation of life and helping them "to see the world through God's eyes and govern their behavior accordingly."

Or, as Andy Ferguson, the Catholic convert, might put it: Americans must learn to submit to Truth. Colson would also agree with Ferguson that submission is a tough sell—at least among Americans who are walking around free. Enter a prison, he continued, and one enters a different evangelical environment, one in which the saving grace of orthodox Christianity is seen at its most brilliant. The Truth that makes one free is most easily grasped by those with little or no freedom.

"The purest form of Christianity is practiced in prisons," Colson agreed, and a primary reason is that prisoners are keenly aware of a core Christian truth: men are not angels. "In prison you don't have to worry about stepping on anyone's toes if you talk about sin. Prisoners know all about sin. As they say, the hangman's noose concentrates the mind."

The promise of the Resurrection, perhaps to no one's surprise, is widely appreciated behind bars. "We showed Mel Gibson's *The Passion of the Christ* in a prison in Broward County, Florida," Colson continued. "This was a woman's prison. It was incredible. Many of these women fell prostrate on the floor. They were crying out to God. They understood that Christ had died for their sins, and how great their sins were. They understood the price Jesus paid. Yes, faith gets pretty serious in prison."

This is not to suggest, he added, that saving souls in prison is easy work. Young black men, who make up a substantial portion of the prison population, can be very difficult to get through to, he explained. "These are feral children, raised in totally desperate circumstances without morally formative communities. They are hostile, angry, and very tough." It is also true, Colson said, that boys who have not known their fathers, or who have little contact with them, are often hostile to belief in God. But there has been an uptick in the number willing to come to meetings, he noted. They are recognizing, as people have recognized since the faith's earliest days, that Christianity offers a haven for the desperate, a community for the dispossessed. Converted prisoners "form a community within a community, a subculture that offers protection."

During my time writing with Colson, I was sometimes surprised by the positions he took on prison reform and other "law-and-order" issues. These could be at great variance with the GOP catechism. When black activists, for example, argued that the draconian penalties for crack cocaine possession were racist, Colson agreed. While law-and-order enthusiasts complained that prisoners have it "too easy" and favored a return to the rock pile, Colson reminded them that someday most of those prisoners would be returning to society and perhaps moving into their neighborhood. If brutalized in prison, they can be expected to brutalize society upon their release. Colson argues that society is best off if criminals are treated humanely and if they convert, which gives them a much better chance of living successfully after release. A 2002 study published by the *Texas Journal of Corrections* underscored the point, finding that faith-based prison programs result in a significantly lower recidivism rate than vocation-based programs—16 percent versus 36 percent (the overall national recidivism rate is nearly 70 percent). Colson also dismays some political operatives by warning believers not to associate themselves too strongly with a political party. He knows better than most how parties can use, and abuse, their various constituencies.

Colson's dedication to "the least of these my brethren" is in keeping with the most profound of Christian traditions. When a white, Boston-bred Ivy Leaguer with stellar Republican credentials takes up the cause of urban black criminals, we are seeing an unlikely alliance—though perhaps a holy alliance. Colson is, in this sense, a contemporary version of one of his Christian heroes, William Wilberforce, who played a key role in the demise of the North African slave trade. Wilberforce was an orthodox Christian who stood against the prevailing intellectual fashions of the day, as expressed by Voltaire, David Hume, and, indeed, the *Encyclopaedia Britannica*, which described blacks this way in its 1797 edition: "Vices the most notorious seem to be the portion of this unhappy race: idleness, treachery, revenge, cruelty, impudence, stealing, lying, profanity, debauchery, nastiness and intemperance are said to have extinguished the principles of natural law, and to have silenced the reproofs of conscience. They are strangers to every sentiment of compassion, and are an awful example of the corruption of man when left to himself." Similar words could be used to describe the general opinion of prisoners today.

Yet Colson sees children of God on the other side of the bars, and in this he reminds me also of Methodist founder John Wesley, whose *Thoughts upon Slavery* (1774) posed a rhetorical question to the captains of slave ships: "Do you never feel another's pain? Have you no sympathy? . . . When you saw the flowing eyes, the heaving breasts, or the bleeding sides or tortured limbs of your fellow beings, were you as a stone or a brute?" One side effect of Colson's Angel Tree Ministry is the reminder of how much suffering results from crime—sin, as Colson might put it—including the suffering of innocents. The program is very popular in middle-class churches and requires teams of volunteers to deliver donated Christmas presents to the children of prisoners. The gifts are presented in the prisoner's name—"This is from your father," a volunteer will say, or, "Your mother wanted you to have this on Christmas morning." These deliveries often take volunteers to parts of town they avoid in both darkness and daylight, and if there is good in realizing the depth of need in our society, then Colson has done immense benefit with this branch of his ministry.

Colson doesn't spend all his time in prisons. He is a social commentator and advocate of what he calls a Christian worldview. He is somewhat notorious for one essay in which he suggested that orthodox Christians are becoming resident aliens in their own countries and questioned how long they can remain loyal citizens of a "regime"—and especially a court system—that undermines traditional Christian morality. Colson did not seem anxious to revisit this controversy, though, like Father John McCloskey, he believes Christians can expect difficulties in the near future. He senses that "it may become illegal to preach against homosexuality." He also remains appalled by the fervor with which abortion has been embraced. "The culture of death placed 800,000 people on the mall not long ago," he said. "That's a reminder of the power wielded by the other side in the culture wars."

I wondered if he thought, as fellow Baptist Richard Land believes, that the pro-life side might well gain enough power to overturn *Roe v. Wade*.

"Well, we're not going to stop trying," he replied. "I think we have a good chance, though the longer it remains constitutional doctrine, the harder it will be to overturn." Scientific advancement, he added, may turn out to play a key role in undermining the decision. When *Roe* was decided, he said, "there was no way to validate when life begins. The Court said it had to be agnostic. Medical technology now makes it easy to detect life in the womb. The right judges could say that technology gives them reason to revisit the case." The *Roe* decision, he added, is losing support, especially among young people. He cited the town of Red Wing, Minnesota, "a town Al Gore carried in 2000," where "the majority of high school students consider themselves pro-life," and a *New York Times* poll that found that support for legalized abortion had dropped among the young "from 48 percent in 1993 to 39 percent today. Clearly, this generation, witnessing the dreadful legacy of abortion, isn't buying pro-choice claims." Like Land, Colson believes that the alliance between evangelicals and conservative Catholics will play an increasingly important role in the culture wars, especially in the campaign against abortion. "This alliance is becoming much stronger. We shed a lot of blood ten years ago when we started out. A lot of supporters abandoned me. But now we get many more plaudits than criticisms. Mainstream evangelicals and orthodox evangelicals are very enthusiastic. That's very important, because if you're fighting for this worldview, we have to stand together."

I closed by asking Colson about the problems he faces when evangelizing outside of prisons. Is preaching to nonprisoners a tougher sell?

"It's a different kind of sale," he replied. "People in prison who are aware of sin and unrighteousness, and who come to believe that God loved them enough to die on the cross, are overwhelmed with gratitude. The greater the sinner, the greater the grace. Outside prison there is often no concept of sin or accountability. People like to believe, 'I'm not a sinner. I'm a good person.' Sin sounds anachronistic."

How do you get past that?

"The classical way is to force people to test the validity of their assumptions about life. You might not be able to sell them a biblical worldview, but you can show them their worldview is a house of cards. For instance, there is a widespread belief that there is no objective truth, that every opinion is as good as every other opinion. So you ask the person you're talking to for their opinion about rape. Is it true, or not true, that people should not be able to rape other people?" Suddenly, he said, one piece of objective truth has been discovered: rape is wrong. Absolutely.

Colson brought up a news story about California Representative Maxine Waters. Rep. Waters had been quoted as saying that she "was sorry her mother didn't have the right to have an abortion." Had she had that right, Colson noted, then Waters might not have ever been born to defend abortion, or any other right.

"Simply put, you have to show people that they can't live with the consequences of their own beliefs." Then they have to be shown that Christianity is both "true" and the only hope for eternal salvation. Christianity, Colson said, "is the only faith that offers redemption." It also "conforms to the way things are. Nothing diagnoses the human condition like the Bible."

His own story, at the very least, does reflect several biblical observations, including the warning that the first shall be last, and vice versa, and that we are unwise to put much faith in princes. Or presidents. His dedication to prisoners reflects a profound submission to the spread of the Word to all corners of the world, including the darkest corners. Of the many high-profile Americans who claim to be "born-again"—which is the title of Colson's book about his great transformation—his case reflects, at least in my view, the fullest sense of what that idea can mean. To put it another way, Colson is an American hero.

I knew another evangelist whose work is not so well known as Chuck Colson's, but in its own way is equally interesting. His mission field is as far from a prison as one is likely to get: one of America's richest neighborhoods, which happens to be located in a part of the country that many orthodox Christians, and Muslims as well, wish would fall into the sea.

Mark Brewer definitely considers himself a missionary, and he may have one of the hardest missions in the world: convincing extremely rich and privileged people that it will be easier to drive a Mercedes through the eye of a needle than for them to enter the Kingdom of Heaven—unless they come to Jesus. Or as he puts it in his easygoing manner, he must convince them that everything they believe is important and everything that gives them status in the world is largely bunk.

Brewer is pastor at Bel Air Presbyterian Church on famed Mulholland Drive in Los Angeles. This was Ronald Reagan's church. Britney Spears has called it her church home, as have Jessica Simpson and her family; her father is active in the Sunday School program. Half of the church's five thousand members, Brewer said, work in the entertainment industry. The church is aligned with the Presbyterian Church USA—the mainstream— but Brewer is a decidedly evangelical Christian minister. As an evangelical, Brewer believes in sin, traditionally understood. He believes in Satan. And he also believes that a person cannot serve both God and Mammon. When he delivers that message, he does so knowing that most of the people listening believe they owe a great deal more to Mammon than God.

"Mammon is much more popular than God in this neighborhood," Brewer began. "There's not a lot of Jesus interest. Spirituality is hip, Jesus is not." Trying to sell a detailed spiritual idea goes against the intellectual grain, as it were. "I like to say that out here you have to dig deep to hit shallow," Brewer said. Mention the name Kierkegaard and most people will probably think he's the creator of a new diet. Shallowness in matters intellectual and spiritual, combined with an obsession with making money, presents forbidding obstacles to the orthodox evangelical. As Brewer put it, he is operating "in the belly of the beast."

Yet while selling Jesus on Mulholland Drive is tough, Brewer draws a good crowd most Sundays. There is much spiritual hunger there, he said. Brewer will not add that he is an extraordinarily gifted preacher, though that is very much the case. In a show-business culture, he can hold his own. And so his Sunday services attract many non-Christians, he said, including Hindus, a large contingent of Jews, agnostics and atheists of various stripes, and even some "watered-down Muslims." A good portion of many of his sermons is spent explaining the differences between the Jewish,

Hindu, Muslim, and Christian approaches to various issues. Then Brewer makes the Christian case.

I asked him how many people respond to his Christian message. That is hard to say, he replied. There is not much "falling out in the spirit" at Bel Air Presbyterian. But he does feel that he is sowing seeds, as well as offering a spiritual harbor for serious Christians. The non-Christians at least are interested enough to show up. Sometimes interest in Christianity's message suddenly becomes intense. One such time was September 11, 2001. In an instant, all the money in Bel Air could not insulate residents from the fear of annihilation. There was much quaking along Mulholland Drive, and Brewer presented his message to full houses.

"Hollywood believes it's a target," Brewer said, adding that in his opinion Hollywood should consider itself a target. "Part of the Islamic anger is directed at this sewer that comes out of the entertainment industry. They don't know how to stop it." Except perhaps with heavy munitions. Tales of mobile nuclear weapons and biological bombs sailing into the port of Los Angeles entered the popular imagination. These contemporary threats heightened interest in the ancient Creed. Or, as Chuck Colson might put it, the hangman entered the room.

September 11 wasn't the first time Brewer had been called on to comfort a congregation reeling from an atrocity. Brewer was pastor at Colorado Community Church the day of the Columbine massacre.

"Columbine helped prepare me for 9/11," Brewer said. In both cases, the killings were premeditated, though totally unexpected by the victims and their survivors. "People have a lot easier time handling deaths that are due to natural disasters," he explained. "In a case like Columbine, you have evil done by the hand of other people," as was also true of the September 11 attacks. Such events raise questions not only about the perpetrators but about the nature of God.

"The message was basically the same for both incidents," Brewer continued. "God didn't cause this. It did not catch God off guard. What you don't do is go up into the pulpit and say that this happened for a greater good. That makes me want to pull my lip over my head. What that says is that God is capricious and cold. It says that God ignores people's feelings. That's not the message. The message is that the first one to cry is God."

I asked how he responds when asked why God would let such terrible things happen. "Why," he said, "is less a question and more a lament. A direct answer is not needed—nor, for that matter, is it available. You just let people keep answering the questions: How do you trust the Lord in a time like this? How do we help those beside us? How do we prevent this in the future?"

Brewer also follows an old show-business maxim: timing is everything. "I have a saying about these kinds of disasters. They are a lot like open-heart surgery. You don't want to close too quickly, but you don't want to leave the wound open too long either." Brewer discussed Columbine over the course of three successive sermons. A central part of his message was the need to deal with the overwhelming anger directed at the killers and the underlying suspicion that more killers were probably ready to strike. "You had to remind people that everyone who plays video games isn't another Dylan Klebold, and that the kids who wear goth clothing are not all homicidal nutcases." There were other pitfalls to avoid, including the attempt to use the incident to advance various beliefs and opinions. "Sainting the beloved is a natural process," he said of the apotheosis of a victim who was said to have professed her faith in God and was then killed for doing so. "That always comes back to haunt you."

Brewer also discussed September 11 in a short series of sermons. As the Hindus and Jews and perhaps a Muslim or two listened, he told the story of Jesus at Lazarus's tomb. It was there that Jesus wept over the curse of death. It is Jesus, he said, who can bring us past death. "You must always bring them back to the promises of God," he said. Thinking of Bill Oudemolen's post-Columbine sermon, I asked Brewer if he dared to bring up Satan to his California congregation, or the idea of evil.

Neither, he said, is off limits.

"There are two ways of looking at evil," Brewer continued. "It's either the lack of something or the presence of something. The Eastern view is that evil is simply a lack of education, a lack of enlightenment. That's pretty much the secular view as well. If we have enough goods, services, and justice, we won't have evil. Like all heresies, there's an element of truth to that. But heresy is truth out of balance." The fullest picture, which is the one he preaches, holds that there is "the presence of a personality behind evil. Is there a presence of evil in the world? I believe history tells us that there absolutely is. And sometimes evil is personified. I'm not saying Harris and Klebold were possessed. I have no idea. But I know they were not innocent of evil. There was something else cooking there beyond them being mad because they were ostracized by jocks." Christian ministers aren't the only ones in Los Angeles who believe in the Devil, Brewer adds. "We've got plenty of Satan worshipers here. They say he was a fallen angel that Christians have given a bad rap."

Christian evangelists do not confront only skepticism, wealth, and perhaps Satan. They must sometimes do battle with other ministers. After Columbine, as Brewer noted, some pastors attempted to draw lifestyle lessons from the attacks or advance pet causes or theories. After September 11, some clergymen famously suggested that God was behind the attacks, which He had de-

ployed as teaching instruments. By this reading, God was the hi-
jackers' co-pilot. Islamic radicals were warm to this idea, but they
were joined by some conservative Christians, most notably the
Rev. Jerry Falwell and the Rev. Pat Robertson, who suggested that
God had withdrawn His protection because of America's increasing tolerance of sin, especially homosexuality. That is Old Testament thinking: God sometimes revealed his displeasure with his
chosen people by allowing their enemies to decimate them.

For other ministers, however, this interpretation was seen not
only as divisive and injurious to the Christian cause, but as simply
wrong. One of the sternest rebukes came from the Rev. Earl F.
Palmer at University Presbyterian Church in Seattle, who insisted
that anyone invoking a vengeful God had missed the entire point
of the Christian faith. Palmer recalled an event he had witnessed
in 1963. The German theologian Karl Barth was lecturing at
Princeton. It happened to be during the time of the trial of Hitler's
henchman Adolf Eichmann. A student rose and asked Barth this
question: "Dr. Barth, now that Adolf Eichmann has been caught,
can we now put the guilt of Germany on his shoulders?" Barth
replied: "No, the guilt of Germany has been placed on quite another man's shoulders." That is the message Christians must live
by, Palmer said. "He has taken our place at the Cross of Calvary
where he has defeated sin and death and the power of all evil, including the devil, by disarming them of their final power. . . . The
fact is that only once did God withdraw his protective boundary
and that was when his Son, Jesus, was alone on the Cross."

That is the basic stage for Christian transformation: a human being alone in the trackless universe, often in pain and perhaps de-
spair, determined if not desperate to find meaning and hope, and
often an answer to death. A human being seeking the omnipotent,

omniscient God—eternally mysterious in His ways, but definitely eternal, in control, and available to those who call on Him. Andy Ferguson looked in an Episcopal seminary but found that God was no longer welcome there. God was waiting for Andy, and Al Regnery, in Rome. Frederica Mathewes-Green heard a voice as she stood before a statue in Dublin, and she and her husband Gary eventually followed that voice into and out of the Episcopal Church and into Orthodoxy. Richard Land, a sixteen-year-old preaching to a Houston congregation, had found God early on, in Scripture, inerrantly presented in his mass-produced Bible. John Tomlin, we can imagine and perhaps pray, found himself in the presence of God as Dylan Klebold took final aim in the Columbine High School library. Charles Colson, broken, shamed, and despised, found himself at the foot of the cross and now carries that hope to lonely men locked away throughout the world.

Then there is the story of Dr. Bernard Nathanson. His search for God started in a lonely place where a common but endlessly sad drama played out. This place was the womb, and the sad drama was innocent life—perhaps reminiscent of another innocent Life— being destroyed. Nathanson, a founder of the abortion rights movement, took his first steps toward the Christian life while watching an ultrasound projection of an abortion, a journey that would eventually take him to Rome. In this he was helped along by Father John McCloskey, who calls Nathanson the "conversion of the century."

At the very least, Nathanson is one of the more unlikely conversions of modern times. Raised an atheistic Jew, by his own count he oversaw sixty thousand abortions, including the abortion of his own son, which Nathanson himself performed. He characterized that abortion as "aseptic and clinical." As a co-founder of the group that became the National Abortion Rights Action League (NARAL), he had successfully battled the church he would later join, again reminiscent of Saint Paul. "Our favorite tack," Nathanson wrote in his autobiography (published by Al Regnery), "was to blame the church for the death of every woman from a botched abortion. There were perhaps three hundred or so deaths from criminal abortions annually in the United States in the sixties, but NARAL in its press releases claimed to have data that supported a figure of five thousand."

His conversion is also somewhat unusual, he wrote, because it was "in reverse."

"The usual and customary progression is belief in God, and His splendid gift of life leads the believer to defend it—and to become pro-life. With me, it was just the opposite: perversely, I journeyed from being pro-life to belief in God."

Ultrasound technology, which he utilized to produce a film called *The Silent Scream* (one of whose more ardent fans was Bel Air Presbyterian Church member Ronald Reagan), showed him, to his satisfaction, that in an abortion a human being is being painfully executed. Technology, however, was not the only factor in his conversion. He was also deeply impressed by the people he encountered at pro-life protests. Demonstrators, he noted, prayed for the victims of abortion, including the women having abortions, policemen, members of the media, and counterprotesters. "They prayed for each other but never for themselves. And I wondered: How can these people give of themselves for a constituency that is (and always will be) mute, invisible, and unable to thank them?"

On December 9, 2000, Nathanson was accepted into the Catholic Church. The ceremony took place in the crypt of St. Patrick's Cathedral in New York. Chuck Colson was there, as were Father John McCloskey and Al Regnery and about fifty other guests. "It was like the first century," Colson told me. "You're down there in the crypt, with its low ceiling, and in comes the cardinal in flowing robes, with a Jew about to be baptized." The late

John Cardinal O'Connor administered the sacraments of Baptism, Confirmation, and Holy Communion. Colson, who recalled the event in a brief essay, was especially moved by Nathanson's sponsor: anti-abortion activist Joan Andrews. "Ironies abound. Joan is one of the pro-life movement's most outspoken warriors, a woman who spent five years in prison for her pro-life activities. It was a sight that burned into my consciousness, because just above Cardinal O'Connor was a cross. . . . I looked at the cross and realized again that what the Gospel teaches is true: in Christ is the victory. He has overcome the world, and the gates of hell cannot prevail against His church. . . . That simple baptism, held without fanfare in the basement of a great cathedral, is a reminder that a holy Baby, born in a stable twenty centuries ago, defies the wisdom of man. He cannot be defeated." But always remember, Colson added, that Christians are called on to advocate an eternal kingdom that is not of this world. That kingdom's ways are its own, and its beliefs— especially regarding sin and the way to salvation—are at odds with modern certainties. The proper role for the Christian is to be the salt of the earth, not its ruler. "When Christians dominated, we created a tyranny. We are probably meant to be countercultural."

Conclusion

The Fish and the Shark

Writing a book about religion can be hazardous to one's spiritual health. The backbiting, dark innuendo, and full-throated denunciations that pass so freely between believers can be much less than inspiring, and here we are talking about believers who share pews in the same denominations. The chasm grows greater between, say, liberal Episcopalians and the staff at the Southern Baptist Theological Seminary. Driving a long stretch of interstate after hearing a Baptist divine rain brimstone upon liberal East Coast clerics, I found myself lapsing into dark contemplations. One might even be inspired to wonder once again what God might have been thinking when He created man.

Well, who knows? What is certain, at least to me, is that writing about religion is a lot more interesting than writing about politics or sports. This is the Big Story, one that the Christian religion promises will come to a righteous conclusion in the fullness of time. At that magic moment, we are assured, the thick veil of ignorance will be lifted. We will no longer look through a glass darkly. All will be revealed. And perhaps, in sports parlance, we shall see whether the liberals or the conservatives win.

This assumption that one day we shall have our answers is one thing about which liberals and conservatives—or, in terms also used throughout this book, progressives and traditionalists—often agree. The metaphor of the lifted veil ended my interviews with both the Rev. Sandra Levy, the liberal Episcopalian, and Dr. Albert Mohler, the grim and thundering Southern Baptist.

It might be recalled that Mohler suggested that the eternal fate of liberal clerics such as the Rev. Levy can be expected to be very grim indeed, while she believes that Jesus would be quite comfortable in her church, with its socially concerned congregation that is also 20 percent gay. In a more optimistic mood, I found myself wondering if both Mohler and Levy might be correct. I certainly hope so. It is a terrible thing to think of the Rev. Levy sharing an eternal berth with the likes of Joseph Stalin or even Courtney Love. There would seem to be no justice in such an arrangement.

Those decisions are, of course, in other hands. But it is worth noting that even people as far apart as Mohler and Levy have common beliefs, including Christianity's central teaching—that Jesus was the Son of God, that He was crucified, that on the third day He rose from the dead, and that those who believe in Him will have everlasting life. Both preach this message, without compromise, from their pulpits. But they are deeply divided on exactly what it means to correctly follow Him, especially His teachings concerning sex. In this, Levy and Mohler reflect not only the divisions found throughout society but the divisions that run between denominations, through denominations, and through the hearts and minds of individual believers. The closer one looks at modern faith, the more shattered it often appears.

Sandra Levy told me people have much trouble "dealing with sex," but they also have a great deal of trouble dealing with religious certitude. This is true not only of liberals but of those who are assumed to accept traditional religious doctrine without reflection. Consider another central issue of faith: who goes to heaven and who goes to hell. "Strait is the gate, and narrow is the way, which leadeth unto life, and few there be that find it"—so warned Jesus, who according to traditional Christian belief is not to be doubted. He was present at the creation, has read the Book of Life cover to cover, and knows how the human drama, and each individual human drama, will turn out. He is not passing along opinions. He is speaking Truth.

Yet as we have seen, His observation—or is it a warning?—about the final destination of most human beings is not warmly received by most American Christians, no matter what church they belong to or how they classify themselves according to their level of religious devotion. The problem with this passage, like many others in the Christian Scriptures, is that it seems so undemocratic, so intolerant, so rigid, so exclusive, and so very hard to square with the popular view of God: a loving, gentle, creative deity whose chief concern is with our happiness and indeed our prosperity. "God is my Co-pilot," the bumper sticker proclaims. God is along for the ride, a steady hand who offers a bit of navigational advice when necessary, takes the wheel while we unwrap our sandwiches, calms turbulence as it arises, and in the end takes us in for a perfect three-point landing in Paradise. The Jesus position—that most people will not go to heaven, which apparently leaves them to languish eternally in hell— is roundly rejected; polling indicates that only 2 percent of Americans believe they are heading in that direction. Forty percent of Americans, let us remember, consider themselves born-again Christians. They may indeed embrace Jesus as their rock and their redeemer, but also stand by their right and privilege to assume that he was mistaken on any number of crucial theological points.

Yet there are crucial differences between believers, differences that are reflected, to some degree, in the types of churches they attend. These differences include competing views of the nature of God and the nature of man. Theological liberals, it seems reasonable to say, assume that God has changed His mind on many matters once thought to be crucial to salvation. He does not stand outside of time or history, demanding strict adherence to a moral code that is the same in every age and for every person. Instead, He appears to have been changed by social developments. In political terms, He has "grown in office." By this view, God is now a good democrat whose greatest hope is to widen His circle and bring as many people to Paradise as will agree to take Him up on His offer of salvation.

This view diverges sharply from the traditional position, which proclaims God as omnipotent, omniscient, and deeply concerned with individual conduct, both physical and mental, as reflected in Jesus's warning that to even think about committing adultery is as bad as the act itself. The traditional God laid down the Law, and to transgress it is to commit sin, and to commit sin is to invite harsh judgment. The reformed God would not be so crass as to intrude in our personal lives at such a level. He is an affirmer, not a judge. If He is all-powerful, He is no longer much inclined to flex His muscles. And as He has taken a lesser role, man's place in the great scheme of things has vastly increased. Man's desires and hopes are now central, as God's once were. This is especially true regarding sex. The traditionalist view of man has it that humans are spiritual beings with sexual impulses that require constant vigilance and restraint. The progressive view holds that humans are sexual creatures with spiritual impulses that require restraint, especially where they threaten personal freedom.

One might assume that the lesser deity, so comforting and so unwilling to be feared, would be the more popular version. We are, after all, living in a freedom-loving age, and we are a freedom-loving people. But as we have seen, that is not the case. If it were, liberal churches would be enjoying the gains seen in more traditional, conservative denominations. Why is this? My own view is that by hollowing out God, liberal theologians created a spiritual vacuum. Their deity is one most Americans cannot respect, much less worship. So they go to churches where that vacuum is filled by traditional religion. While often ignorant of the fine points of doctrine and in some instances at odds with it, Americans believe in overwhelming numbers that God is omnipotent and, as one survey found, that He "rules the world." They could not find that God in liberal churches. The God they desire, and whom they sense is Real, is mysterious, all-powerful, and worthy of worship. He requires submission. He insists that there is such a thing as sin, and He requires that individuals conform their lives to the ancient code if they desire the best of possible outcomes. This God best addresses the "unease" that William James tells us is a central characteristic of the religious personality. And only this sometimes harsh, mysterious, demanding God, it might be added, seems to find a reflection in the harsh, mysterious, and astoundingly beautiful universe we find ourselves living in. This is the God of the past, and He seems to also be the God of the future. His ways are imperfectly followed, but only He is worth following.

As we also found, most traditionalist believers are not the creatures typically portrayed in the popular media. They are often said to have "retreated" into orthodox belief as a way of escaping the vicissitudes of modern life. What is not said is that such a "retreat" makes great demands and many of these believers assume that they have taken the path of greatest resistance.

These traditionalists, I found, are nearly alone in reminding a visitor that the Christian Creed is not to be mistaken for the work of romantic poets. It is a Creed that will separate father from son, wife from husband, and children from parents.

They believe themselves to be members of a small, isolated, and increasingly endangered community. Father John McCloskey says that only 10 percent of Catholics are "with the program," by which he means that they attend Mass and Confession regularly and adhere closely to church teachings. That same number was mentioned by several Protestants, including Albert Mohler, in regard to the number of Christians who live by the demands of the traditional faith. Father McCloskey, who is highly admired by many serious Catholics, warns that deeply committed Christians will face severe and sometimes murderous persecution in the fairly near future. The point is not to endorse these apprehensions but to acknowledge that this type of believer embraces his faith despite the suspicion, and in some cases the expectation, that fidelity may cost him his life. These believers do homage to a Savior who bought their salvation at a high price and warned that their personal victories will not come on the cheap.

They certainly see the storm clouds gathering. Their children can no longer pray before football games or receive public scholarships to pursue religious studies. Every time they turn on the television they encounter one hideous blasphemy or another. When they glance at a car bumper, they may see one of those Darwin footed fish or an emblem of a shark eating a Christian fish. Or they may see a bumper sticker proclaiming, "Non Judgment Day Is Coming," and know that many Americans, including many religious ones, hope for that day. They see this not as a call for neutrality but as a rejection of the moral codes that have flowed from traditional Christianity, codes that are increasingly perceived as nefarious and malevolent restraints on individual freedom. These believers sense that they are losing ground and that the loss will have catastrophic effects beyond their own persecution.

The decline of traditional faith in Europe, as Father John McCloskey reminds us, has been accompanied by negative population growth. The U.S. population is held steady by immigration, he added. (He blamed contraception and abortion, which he holds as rejections of Christian teaching, for this "holocaust.") In a somewhat similar vein, Bernard Lewis, perhaps our era's preeminent scholar of Islam, caused a major upheaval in 2004 by proclaiming that Europe would be Islamic by the end of this century, "at the latest." This is not something Lewis, a secular scholar, hopes for, but something he expects. Islam is expanding rapidly into Europe and filling the vacuum created by the collapse of traditional Christianity. There are around fifty thousand conversions to Islam in France each year, for example, and in 2004 the number of people attending weekly services in mosques exceeded the number of those attending the services of the Church of England. Secularism, the result of the shark eating the fish, does not create a steady secular state. It creates a spiritual vacuum that will be filled by a more dynamic faith.

Islam, however, is not everyone's favorite choice as the default religion. Philip Jenkins, whose work was discussed in chapter 4, argues—as does Father Richard John Neuhaus—that secularism is in decline and that the most dynamic religion is not Islam but Christianity.

And not liberal Christianity. "Worldwide," Jenkins writes, "Christianity is actually moving toward supernaturalism and neo-orthodoxy, and in many ways toward the ancient world view expressed in the New Testament: a vision of Jesus as the embodiment of divine power, who overcomes the evil forces that inflict calamity and sickness upon the human race." His legions, Jenkins adds, are massive and growing rapidly. The Christian population is 480 million in Latin America, 360 million in Africa, and 313 million in Asia. Pentecostals, never to be mistaken for theological liberals, now number around 400 million, and that number could rise to one billion by midcentury. By comparison, the Christian population of North America is around 260 million. The results are, of course, uncertain, but this change in the demographic balance will result, Jenkins says, in an interesting development: the next time a papal election takes place, more than 40 percent of the voting cardinals will be from the south, and soon after that they will constitute a majority.

Father McCloskey looks into the future and expects mayhem, as does Albert Mohler. Then again, Southern Baptist Richard Land concluded our interview by saying of his liberal opponents: "I'd rather be playing our hand than theirs." Not all Christian traditionalists think alike, as has often been suggested, even those who work in the same building.

As mentioned in the introduction, I began this book as an itinerant Presbyterian. I remain such. This is no major accomplishment. While I was often asked, especially by priests and ministers, what my religious bearing might be, no one I interviewed for this book attempted to sign me up. Father McCloskey came the closest, e-mailing me that "Christ wants us all in the same fold," but that was the last word from him on the matter. For better or worse, I remain an enthusiastic fan of Christian consumerism, as it is sometimes pejoratively called. To return one last time to economic terms, I like having several brands to choose from. Perhaps one day a light will go off and I will darken some majestic door. I don't imagine I'll end up in Rome, or as a Unitarian. I have developed a soft spot for women priests and at the same time have little interest in modern art, the presentation of which seems to be the Unitarians' lone forte. The Orthodox Church was a pleasant surprise, and one I would quickly suggest to anyone seeking a fairly dramatic departure from ordinary Protestantism. With knees and ankles worn down by years of running, however, I have to think twice about all that standing.

In the meantime, religion continues to be the Story of Stories, one that encompasses history as well as contemporary life and guides to some degree our view of what the future might hold. Taken all together, it is often a troubling story, full of conflict, persecution, bloodshed, and the occasional bout of international mayhem. Many a sword has been sharpened while nearby someone whistled a hymn.

But the story also has hopeful chapters, some of them breath-taking, some coming from unexpected places. As I concluded this chapter, a story came across the wires from the *Guardian*, written by Jason Burke. It concerned the spiritual transformation of some surviving members of the Pol Pot regime. Pol Pot, of course, is held guilty of ordering the murder of several million Cambodians. Though some of us hope devoutly that there is no hell, for his case we make an exception.

Burke reported that hundreds of Pol Pot's former fighters have been baptized by evangelicals over the past year in the southwest mountain city of Pailin, which has "four churches, all with pastors and growing congregations. At least 2,000 of those who followed Pol Pot, the guerrillas' former leader who died six years ago, now worship Jesus." Seven of ten of these converts, according to a local pastor, took part in the extermination and forced-labor campaign.

There was a quote from one convert, now in his fifties: "When I was a soldier I did bad things. I don't know how many we killed. We were following orders and thought it was the right thing to do. I read the Bible and I know it will free me from the weight of the sins I have committed." Thus the old-time religion gained a new refugee. Thus another hard journey leads to the foot of the ancient cross.

Index